AN INTRODUCTION TO
OLD ENGLISH

AN INTRODUCTION TO
OLD ENGLISH

by

G. L. BROOK

*Professor of English Language and Medieval English Literature
in the University of Manchester*

MANCHESTER
UNIVERSITY PRESS

© G. L. Brook, 1955
Published by Manchester University Press
Oxford Road, Manchester M13 9PL

Reprinted 1962, 1966, 1974, 1978
ISBN 0 7190 0569 8

PRINTED IN GREAT BRITAIN BY
UNWIN BROTHERS LIMITED
THE GRESHAM PRESS, OLD WOKING, SURREY

TO
MY WIFE

CONTENTS

PREFACE

In writing this book I have had in mind primarily the needs of First Year university students reading for an Honours degree in English. It is hoped that students whose interests are mainly philological will find here an introduction to more advanced works, but my chief concern has been with those who, without intending to become specialists in Old English, wish to acquire enough knowledge of the grammar to enable them to read Old English texts. A certain amount of memory-work is inevitable, but this has been reduced to a minimum and, as far as possible, I have tried not only to describe what happened but to explain why it happened. Books on Old English grammar often make the subject needlessly difficult by treating it as the development of primitive Germanic rather than as the ancestor of Modern English ; I have made mention of only such sound-changes as are necessary to explain the variations that occur in Old English texts, omitting such topics as Ablaut and Grimm's Law as unsuitable for beginners.

Five short prose extracts have been included, in the belief that the study of any language should from the beginning be closely related to the study of texts, but the book is intended primarily as a grammar rather than a reader, and it is hoped that students will find that the amount of grammar included will enable them to read the extracts in readers like those of Wyatt and Sweet or the texts in Methuen's Old English Library. The prose extracts are given in approximately chronological order ; for those who wish to read them in ascending order of difficulty, I suggest the order : 3, 4, 5, 2, 1. Since I hope that all who use this book will have some interest in the historical development of English during the Old English period as well as afterwards, I have made no attempt to re-write the texts in early West Saxon, and they have all been collated with the manuscripts or with micro-films. When it has seemed necessary to emend the text, the manuscript reading is given in a footnote. In order to help beginners with the identification of forms, I have added fairly full explanatory notes and a glossary with frequent cross-references.

In spite of the brevity of the book, the list of those to whom I am indebted is a formidable one. I owe something to all the authors whose books are listed in the Bibliography, but I should like to make special acknowledgement of my indebtedness to Miss E. E. Wardale's *Old English Grammar*, and to the excellent section on syntax in Sweet's *Anglo-Saxon Primer*, revised by Professor Norman Davis. For permission to reproduce the frontispiece and the prose extracts I am indebted to the Keeper of Western MSS. of the Bodleian Library, the Cambridge University Librarian, the Master and Fellows of Corpus Christi College, Cambridge and the Trustees of the British Museum. I am grateful for the help that I have received from Miss P. C. Horne and Miss L. D. Hourani. Greatest of all is my debt to Professor Bruce Dickins, Professor Simeon Potter, Mr. R. M. Wilson, Dr. F. E. Harmer, Mr. R. F. Leslie, and my wife, all of whom read the book in typescript or in proof and allowed me to profit by their experience as teachers of Old English. The responsibility for mistakes is my own.

G. L. BROOK

June, 1954

PREFACE TO THE SECOND EDITION

I SHOULD like to take this opportunity of thanking the students, reviewers and colleagues who have suggested the changes which I have made in the present edition. I am particularly indebted to Professor M. L. Samuels for the corrections included in his review in *The Review of English Studies*, to Mr. John Braidwood for the comments which he sent to me privately, and, above all, to my colleague Dr. R. F. Leslie for the patience and thoroughness with which he has checked and corrected the first edition of this book.

G. L. B.

November 1961

ABBREVIATIONS

acc.	accusative	OE.	Old English
adj.	adjective	OHG.	Old High German
adv.	adverb	ON.	Old Norse
Ang.	Anglian	ONhb.	Old Northumbrian
cj.	conjunction	OS.	Old Saxon
comp.	comparative	part.	participle
dat.	dative	pl.	plural
dem.	demonstrative	poss.	possessive
f.	feminine	pp.	past participle
gen.	genitive	ppl.	participial
Gmc.	Germanic	prep.	preposition
IE.	Indo-European	pres.	present
imper.	imperative	pret.	preterite
impers.	impersonal	prim.	primitive
ind.	indicative	pron.	pronoun
infin.	infinitive	reflex.	reflexive
instr.	instrumental	sb.	substantive
interj.	interjection	sing.	singular
interr.	interrogative	subj.	subjunctive
Kt.	Kentish	superl.	superlative
m.	masculine	sv.	strong verb
ME.	Middle English	v.	verb
MnE.	Modern English	w.	with
n.	neuter	WGmc.	West Germanic
Nhb.	Northumbrian	WS.	West Saxon
nom.	nominative	wv.	weak verb
num.	numeral		

* indicates that the form which follows is not recorded in the texts that have been preserved.

Symbols within square brackets are phonetic symbols; for the most part they are the ' broad ' symbols of the International Phonetic Association.

Vowel-length is indicated by a horizontal stroke above the letter. An acute accent is used to indicate that a vowel was lengthened in late Old English (§ 64 (*f*)).

INTRODUCTION

1. Old English, or Anglo-Saxon, is the name given to the language spoken in Britain by the Germanic settlers from the time of the earliest settlements in the fifth century until the end of the eleventh century. Like all living languages, Old English was changing during the whole period of its history, but during the eleventh century, partly as a result of the Norman Conquest, the rate of change was quickened, and it is convenient to regard a new period, known as Middle English, as extending from the twelfth to the fifteenth century. Old English is worthy of study partly because it is the language in which English literature is written for the first three or four centuries of its recorded history and partly because of the light it throws on the later development of the English language.

2. A knowledge of English literature that does not include Old English writings is seriously incomplete, for English literary tradition is unbroken from the time of the earliest recorded prose and verse down to the present day. When compared with most other European literatures, English literature is remarkable for the early date from which texts of real literary value have been preserved. Chaucer is sometimes described as the father of English literature, but it is well to remember that in date Chaucer comes rather later than half-way in the chronological stream of English literature that has been preserved. The persistent influence of Old English can be seen in the themes and images from Old English poetry which have been used by later English writers. In a letter to Robert Bridges, dated 26 November 1882, Gerard Manley Hopkins wrote, ' In fact I am learning Anglo-saxon and it is a vastly superior thing to what we have now '. In his enthusiasm Hopkins no doubt over-stated the truth, but students of Old English poetry will see the connection between this statement and the ' sprung rhythm ' of Hopkins's poetry. English verse is based on stress, not on the number of syllables in a line, and this accentual system, fundamental to English poetry, is an inheritance from Old English, a deep-rooted native technique which has survived military invasion and the influence of foreign literary fashions.

Old English texts cannot be read satisfactorily in Modern English versions. Modern renderings of the poetic texts share the defects of all translations of poetry; they cannot simultaneously convey both the elaborate and sophisticated verse-structure and the full implications of the meaning of the original. One of the characteristics of Old English poetry is the compression of a complex image into a single compound word; the sense of these compounds can be brought out in translation only at the expense of losing the terseness and bite of the original.

Although Old English poetry is more varied than it seems to be at first, it is for the most part dignified, mature and serious, often to the point of melancholy. Much of it preserves a scheme of values belonging to the pre-Christian Germanic outlook on life; loyalty and fortitude are seen as the qualities to be most praised and most demanded. Some of the later poetry shows these ideals taken over into the pattern of thought of a well-established Christian society. *The Battle of Maldon*, a poem written to commemorate a valiant but disastrous English encounter with the Danes in 991, illustrates the assimilation of the heroic code into Christian belief.

Old English prose lacks the high stylistic achievement of the verse, but its qualities should not be underrated. At its best it has the virtues and the defects of colloquial speech: it is alive but is sometimes obscure. Words have not lost their freshness through over-use. The simplicity for which more self-conscious art often strives hard is achieved by the Old English prose-writer naturally and without effort.

It is true of the prose, as of the poetry, that modern English versions cannot satisfactorily replace the original. Old English has not the same syntax as Modern English, and when its sentences are made to conform to modern patterns the vigour of the original is lost.

3. Just as Old English literature is of interest both for its own sake and for the help it affords to the study of later literature, so the study of the Old English language has a double value, as an indispensable preliminary to the study of Old English literature and as an aid to the study of the history of the English language and of later English literature. Although there has been no break in the continuity of development of the English language from the earliest times, there have been so many changes that the earliest texts can be read only by those who have made a study of Old English. A knowledge of Old English is a less obvious, though still considerable, help to the student of later English literature. There are innumerable examples in the works of Shakespeare and Milton of words which are liable to be misunderstood by a modern reader because they are used in a sense closer to the etymological sense than that current today. Since Latin and French are commonly taught in schools whereas Old English is not, readers of today are more likely to recognize the changes in meaning of foreign loan-words into English than those of native words. The words that are most likely to be misunderstood by a reader of Shakespeare's plays are not the unfamiliar words like *yare* (OE. **gearu,** *ready*) or *to ear* (OE. **erian,** *to plough*), but those which are current today with changed meanings or which resemble other words which would fit the Shakespearean context. The reader is in danger of substituting a different image for the one intended by the author, and the dictionary offers no help because the reader unfamiliar with the earlier history of the language is not conscious that a problem exists. Two examples must suffice. When Macbeth says, 'If thou speak'st false, Upon the next tree shalt thou hang alive Till Famine cling thee' (*Macbeth*, v. v. 40), he is using *cling* with the meaning 'shrivel up', a sense closely related to the usual Old English meaning but not current today. Again, when Timon says, 'Destruction fang mankind' (*Timon of Athens*, iv. iii. 23) he does not use *fang* in the sense 'to strike one's fangs into'; this verb is not recorded before the nineteenth century. He is using a verb *fang* meaning 'to seize', no longer in current use but very familiar to students of Old English in the form **fōn, pp. gefangen.**

The help offered by Old English is not confined to the meaning of words. The confusion which many people today experience in the use of the verbs *lie* and *lay* is lessened when the two verbs are traced back to Old English, where the preterite of the strong verb is not, as it unfortunately is in Modern English, identical with the infinitive of the weak verb. The word *moe* is of frequent occurrence in Shakespeare. The student who is familiar with OE. **mā,** *more*, as well as **māra,** *greater*, is in no danger of assuming, as many editors have done, that *moe* is a mistake for *more* which must be emended.

4. Some students are attracted to Old English by its historical interest. There is an undoubted gain in vividness as well as in authenticity when we read King Alfred's account of the state of learning in England in the words which he himself used instead of in a modern translation. The vocabulary of Old English illustrates the influence of Christianity in the adaptation of pagan ideas to Christian uses. The *Anglo-Saxon Chronicle* shows the development of Old English prose style from the bare recording of facts to a pungent narrative technique. From the ninth century onwards a personal note breaks into the annals. In the description of the battles between the English and the Danes, the English army is always the **fyrd**; the Danish army is the **here,** a word with derogatory implications, connected with the verb **hergian,** *to harry.* Modern English translators of the *Chronicle* find it hard to reproduce this economical verbal distinction between the English and Danish forces. Similarly, a modernized version cannot adequately reproduce the lively indignation of the chroniclers of the turn of the eleventh century when they express their exasperation at the ineptitudes of military strategy under King Ethelred.

5. Most of the languages of Europe and many of the languages of Asia are descended from a single pre-historic language known as Indo-European. This language split up into a number of groups, each of which has some linguistic features that are not shared by the other groups. They include Indo-Iranian, Armenian, Albanian, Greek, Balto-Slavonic, Italic, Celtic and Germanic. The Germanic group of languages split into three sub-divisions:

East Germanic. The only representative of any importance is Gothic. This is now a dead language, but fairly extensive remains of a fourth-century translation of parts of the Bible into Gothic have been preserved. Because of their early date, Gothic forms often throw useful light on the earlier history of Old English words, but it is important not to confuse Gothic with primitive Germanic. No Old English words were derived from Gothic. Gothic forms are quoted in Old English grammars in order to throw light on the Germanic forms from which both the Gothic and the Old English words are derived.

North Germanic, or Scandinavian, is represented today by Icelandic, Norwegian, Swedish, Danish, and Faroese. A valuable literature, both in prose and verse, has come down to us written in Old Icelandic.

West Germanic is represented today by German, Dutch, Flemish, Frisian and English. The oldest form of German is known as Old High German. Other early West Germanic languages which are useful for comparison with Old English are Old Saxon and Old Frisian. The latter, of all the West Germanic languages, most closely resembles Old English, and the two languages are sometimes grouped together and said to be derived from Anglo-Frisian.

6. Dialectal differences are to be found in all Old English texts. There are not enough localized Old English texts surviving to make it possible for us to draw precise boundary lines between the various dialects, but four main dialects can be distinguished in Anglo-Saxon England, apart from the western districts, Cornwall, Wales and Strathclyde, where Celtic languages were spoken. The chief Old English dialects were:

(*a*) **West Saxon,** the dialect spoken in the old kingdom of Wessex, which included most of England south of the Thames with the exception of Kent and Cornwall.

(*b*) **Kentish,** the dialect of the Jutes, who settled in Kent and part of the neighbouring counties as well as in the Isle of Wight and a strip of the opposite coast of Hampshire.

(*c*) **Mercian,** the dialect spoken between the Thames and the Humber, especially in the western part of that area. So far as we can judge from the scanty evidence, East Anglia had a different dialect.

(*d*) **Northumbrian,** the dialect spoken north of the Humber.

Mercian and Northumbrian had many points in common, and they are sometimes grouped together as Anglian. Under King Alfred the West Saxon dialect achieved greater importance than the other Old English dialects, and most of the Old English literature which has survived is written in West Saxon, though some Anglian forms occur in nearly all Old English texts. West Saxon is therefore the dialect which can most usefully form the basis of a study of Old English, though it must be remembered that modern Standard English has developed from the East Midland dialect of Middle English, which was descended from an Anglian dialect. Such modern English words as *cold, cheese* and *hear* are descended from Anglian and not from West Saxon forms.

SPELLING

7. The Old English alphabet was based on a Celtic variety of the Latin alphabet with the addition of two letters borrowed from the runic alphabet, a form of writing used by the Germanic peoples for inscriptions. One of these letters represented [w] ; the other, þ (thorn), represented [θ] or [ð]. A third new letter was devised by putting a stroke through d, and this ' crossed d ' (đ or ð) was used, like runic þ, to denote both [θ] and [ð]. While some grammars adopt the convention of using þ to represent the voiceless consonant and keeping ð to represent the voiced sound, others use þ initially and ð in other positions, but in most Old English manuscripts the two letters appear to be interchangeable.

Several of the letters used in Anglo-Saxon manuscripts differ in shape from those now current, and older printed editions of Old English texts often used special type to imitate them. The usual practice today, however, is to avoid the use of special type as far as possible, but most editions of Old English texts make use of the letters þ, ð and the ligatures æ and œ.

8. Vowel-length is generally not indicated in manuscripts, though we find in Old English the beginnings of the device with which we are familiar today of doubling a vowel to show that it is long, as in MnE. *food*. The accents which are sometimes written above vowels in Old English manuscripts may have been intended to indicate vowel-length but they may also have been used to indicate stress. In grammars and in many editions of Old English texts vowel-length is generally indicated, as in the present grammar, by a horizontal line above long vowels and the accented elements of long diphthongs. It is important to notice the length of a vowel, because many sound-changes affect long vowels while leaving short vowels unaffected and *vice versa*. Hence, from the point of view of the later development of English words, the difference between a and ā is as important as the difference between a and e. In the study of Old English versification, too, a knowledge of vowel-length is important, and noting the difference of vowel-length is a useful way of distinguishing between words that superficially resemble each other, such as wīg, *war*, and **wiga**, *warrior;* **wīn**, *wine*, and **wine**, *friend;* **mān**, *evil*, and **man(n)**, *man*.

9. Old English spelling is on the whole more consistent than that of Modern English, but it is not completely phonetic. It is important, but not always easy, to decide whether variations in spelling reflect variations in pronunciation or whether the variant spellings are simply different ways of representing the same sound. For example, in late Old English, **k** is sometimes used as a spelling for **c** when it represents a velar plosive (§ 13(*d*)). An example of a spelling convention is the insertion of an **e** between **sc, g,** or **c** and a following back vowel in such words as **sc(e)acan,** *to shake;* **fēog(e)an,** *to hate;* **þenc(e)an,** *to think.* In such words the **e** may well have been a device to indicate that the preceding consonant was palatal, and **scacan** and **sceacan** were probably pronounced alike. There were no silent consonants in Old English. Thus, four consonants were pronounced in OE. **cniht,** *boy*, instead of two as in its Modern English equivalent *knight*. Another way in which Old English spelling gives a truer picture of the pronunciation than that of Modern English is that double consonants, except when they occurred finally, were pronounced as double, whereas in Modern English they have generally been simplified. Today double consonants are pronounced as such only in compound words where the final consonant of the first element is the same as the initial consonant of the second element. Hence the medial consonants of OE. **bucca,** *he-goat*, and **willan,** *to desire*, were pronounced like the medial consonants of Modern English *book-case* and *ill-luck*.

10. When a sound-change took place (§ 15), the change was sometimes, but not always, recorded in spelling. Hence, after a sound-change had taken place there often occurred side by side two different forms of the same word, one with a spelling representing the old pronunciation and one with a more phonetic spelling representing the new pronunciation. When the resultant variation in spelling was extended to other words in which the sound-change in question did not take place, an *inverted spelling* is said to occur. For example, in the course of the Old English period **g** disappeared after **i** with compensatory lengthening of the vowel (§ 64(*e*)). Hence we find such spellings as **dysī,** *foolish*, side by side with old spellings like **dysig.** As a result of the existence of two ways of representing the same sound, **ī** and **ig** came to be interchangeable, and we find **ig** used as a spelling for **ī** in **hig,**

nom. pl. of the 3rd personal pronoun, and in **big** beside **bī,** *by,* where there is no etymological justification for the **g.** The forms **hig** and **big** are thus said to be inverted spellings. Similarly, **ie** had been monophthongized to **ĭ** by the time of King Alfred (§ 40), with the result that in some manuscripts **ie** is used as a spelling for **i** in such words as **hieder,** *hither.*

PRONUNCIATION

11. Old English vowels were pronounced approximately as follows:

a was a back open vowel [ɑ]. An English speaker can most readily acquire the correct pronunciation by shortening the vowel which he uses in *father,* as in **habban,** *to have.*

ā was pronounced [ɑ:], like the **a** in MnE. *father,* as in **hām,** *home.*

æ was a front open vowel [æ], like the **a** in MnE. *bad,* as in **æcer,** *field.*

ǣ was the same sound lengthened [æ :]. It was nearly like the first element of the diphthong heard in MnE. *there,* as in **pǣr,** *there.*

e was a front half-close vowel [e], nearly like the first element of the diphthong heard in MnE. *gate,* as in **settan,** *to set.*

ē was the same sound lengthened [e :], as in **grēne,** *green.*

i was a front close vowel [i], nearly like the **i** in MnE. *sit,* as in **sittan,** *to sit.*

ī was pronounced [i :], like the **i** in MnE. *machine,* as in **rīdan,** *to ride.*

o was a back half-close vowel [o], nearly like the first element of the diphthong heard in MnE. *bøne,* as in **god,** *god.*

ō was the same sound lengthened [o :], as in **gōd,** *good.*

u was a back close vowel [u], like the **u** in MnE. *full,* as in **munuc,** *monk.* It was never pronounced [ʌ] like the **u** in MnE. *run.*

ū was pronounced [u :], like the **oo** in MnE. *fool,* as in **hūs,** *house.*

y was a front close rounded vowel [y], like the **u** in French **tu,** as in **cynn,** *kin.*

ȳ was the same sound lengthened [y :], as in **hȳdan,** *to hide.*

œ was a front half-close rounded vowel [ø], like the French vowel in **peu,** as in *œxen, oxen.*

ōœ was the same sound lengthened [ø :], as in **dōōma(n),** *to judge.* The sounds **œ, ōœ** did not normally occur in WS.

12. The diphthongs were pronounced as written except that the first element of **ēa** was [ɛ :] or [æ :], not [e:]. They were generally falling diphthongs; that is to say the stress was on the first element. In long diphthongs the length-mark is generally placed over only the accented element. Examples are **heard,** *hard;* **bēam,** *tree;* **weorpan,** *to throw;* **cēosan,** *to choose;* **liornian,** *to learn;* **fīond,** *enemy;* **giefan,** *to give;* **hīeran,** *to hear.*

13. The consonants **b, d, l, m, n, p, t, w,** and **x** were pronounced as in Modern English. The other consonants call for special comment:

(*a*) When **f, s** and **þ (ð)** occurred medially between voiced sounds, provided that they were not doubled, they were voiced; that is to say they were pronounced [v], [z], and [ð]. In other positions they were voiceless, and were pronounced [f], [s], and [θ]. It is possible that **f** represented a bi-labial fricative in Old English, whereas today it is a labio-dental fricative. Examples of the voiced pronunciation are: **giefan,** *to give;* **wulfas,** *wolves;* **cēosan,** *to choose;* **bōsm,** *bosom;* **baþian,** *to bathe;* **eorþe,** *earth.* Examples of the voiceless pronunciation are: **wulf,** *wolf;* **pyffan,** *to puff;* **standan,** *to stand;* **hūs,** *house;* **þencan,** *to think;* **moþþe,** *moth.*

(*b*) **h** was an aspirate, pronounced [h], as in MnE. *hut,* initially before vowels and in the groups **hl, hn, hr,** and (except in Nhb.) **hw,** as in **habban,** *to have;* **hlūd,** *loud;* **hnesce,** *soft;* **hring,** *ring.* Initially in the group **hw** in Nhb., and medially and finally in all dialects, except after front vowels, **h** was a voiceless velar fricative [x], like the **ch** in Scots *loch* or German **noch,** as in **hwæt,** *what;* **eahta,** *eight;* **furh,** *furrow;* **scōh,** *shoe.* Medially and finally after front vowels it was a palatal fricative [ç], like the **ch** in German **ich,** as in **siehþ,** *he sees;* **hliehhan,** *to laugh.*

(*c*) **r** was trilled [r] initially, as in modern Scots, but before consonants and finally it was a fricative. Examples are: **rīdan,** *to ride;* **word,** *word;* **ēr,** *before.*

(*d*) Initially before consonants, initially and medially before back vowels or secondary front vowels (§ 83) and finally after consonants or back vowels, OE. **c** was a velar plosive [k], like the **c** in MnE. *cool.* Examples are: **cnēo,** *knee;* **cuman,** *to come;* **cyssan,** *to kiss;* **sprecan,** *to speak;* **þancian,** *to thank;* **weorc,** *work;* **bōc,** *book.* Next to primary front vowels and in the palatal group **nc,** early OE. **c** was usually pronounced like the **k** in MnE. *kid;* by the end of the Old English period it had become an affricative consonant [tʃ], pronounced like MnE. **ch,** as in **cēosan,** *to choose;* **bēc,** *books;* **benc,** *bench.* By the end of the Old English period **sc** had generally come to be pronounced [ʃ], like MnE. **sh,** as in **sceolde,** *should;* **fisc,** *fish.*

(*e*) Initially before consonants, back vowels and secondary front vowels, and in the group **gg,** OE. **g** was a velar plosive [g], like the **g** in MnE. *good,* as in **glæd,** *glad;* **gōd,** *good;* **gēs,** *geese;* **singan,** *to sing;* **frogga,** *frog.*

Medially after back vowels **g** was a voiced velar fricative [ɣ]. Finally after back vowels, **r** or **l** it was probably unvoiced to [x], pronounced like the **ch** in Scots *loch.* Examples are : **fugol,** *bird;* **plōg,** *a measure of land;* **burg,** *town.*

Initially before front vowels and medially and finally after front vowels, **g** was a palatal fricative [j], like the **y** in MnE. *yield,* as in **giefan,** *to give;* **fæger,** *fair;* **dæg,** *day.* When this sound represents Gmc. [j], it is occasionally spelt **i,** as in **iū** beside **geō,** *formerly;* **iung** beside **geong,** *young* (§ 83(*b*)).

The group **cg** represented a double palatalized **g.** By the end of the Old English period it had probably acquired the sound [dʒ], like the **dg** in MnE. *edge,* as in **hrycg,** *back;* **secgan,** *to say.*

When the group **ng** was preceded by a back vowel the **g** was a velar plosive like the **g** in MnE. *longer,* as in **hungor,** *hunger;* **lang,** *long.* When the **ng** was preceded by a front vowel the **g** was a palatal plosive nearly like the **g** in MnE. *finger,* as in **lengra,** *longer;* **þing,** *thing.*

STRESS

14. In uncompounded words the chief stress fell on the stem-syllable, which is usually the first syllable, as in **beran,** *to carry;* **maþelode,** *he spoke.* Compound words whose second element was a noun or an adjective generally had the chief stress on the first element; compound words whose second element was a verb generally came to have the chief stress on the second element, a change which was brought about by the existence of compound verbs side by side with simple verbs. Hence 'andgiet, *understanding*, beside on'gietan, *to understand;* 'andsaca, *adversary*, beside on'sacan, *to strive against*. Nouns and adjectives formed from, or closely associated with, verbs generally agreed with verbs in having the chief stress on the second syllable, and the prefix ge- was always lightly stressed. Examples are be'bod, *command;* be'hēfe, *suitable;* ge'sceaft, *creation;* ge'mǣne, *common*. In compound adverbs the more important element had the chief stress, as 'ealneg (from [ealne weg), *always*, beside on'weg, *away*.

PHONOLOGY

15. All living languages are constantly changing, and phonology is the branch of linguistic study which deals with the changes which sounds undergo. The chief value of the study of sound-changes to a student of Old English is that such a study enables him to understand the reasons for the large number of variant forms of the same word or of related words which occur in texts ; he knows what variations to expect, and the amount of unreasoning memory work which he finds necessary is lessened.

Sound-changes have been taking place in English at every period of its history, but as a rule we do not notice them because they take place very gradually, and because for the last few hundred years they have not been reflected in the written language.

When sound-changes are mentioned it should always be remembered that speech is an action of individuals and that no two people speak in exactly the same way. Slight eccentricities in the pronunciation of an individual will generally not be noticed and may in time be corrected by the speaker, but identical variations from the norm that occur in the speech of a large number of speakers may in time come to be accepted by the majority of the speakers of a given community. When this happens, a sound-change is said to have taken place. A frequent cause of sound-change is a tendency towards greater ease of pronunciation, but the desire to preserve intelligibility prevents the process from going too far. Sound-changes such as the assimilation of consonants (§ 90) are examples of the tendency towards ease of pronunciation, but not all the Old English sound-changes can be explained in this way. It is always desirable to consider the phonetic basis of a sound-change in terms of the movements of the organs of speech. By doing so and by comparing Old English forms with those in cognate languages, it is often possible to reconstruct forms which we know must once have existed even though they are not recorded in texts. For example, it is fairly safe to say that **slēan,** *to strike,* was earlier ***slahan.** When such forms are given in grammars they are generally preceded by an asterisk, a conventional sign to show that they are hypothetical.

Sound-changes may be classified as independent (or isolative) and dependent (or combinative). Changes of the first class affect a given sound of a language at a given time and place whatever the neighbouring sounds may be; changes of the second class are dependent on the neighbouring sounds. These two kinds of change are exemplified by sound-changes which are taking place in English at the present day. The tendency to make the first element of the diphthong in words like *day* more open is an independent change; the lengthening of the **o** sometimes heard in *off* and *coffee* is the result of a dependent change. In Old English, fronting of **ā** (§§ 27, 28) is an independent change, whereas front mutation (§ 39) is a dependent change.

16. The regular operation of sound-changes is often disturbed by the influence of analogy. In its linguistic sense, analogy consists of the modification of the form of a word because of association with other words. The essential difference between sound-change and analogy is that the former is a gradual development while the latter is a sudden replacement. The effect of analogy is generally to smooth out the irregularities in a language, and it affects both phonology and accidence. An example of analogical interference with sound-change is to be found in the genitive singular of **pæþ,** *path.* The regular form is **pæþes,** but an analogical form **paþes** also occurs as a result of the influence of the plural forms, such as nom. pl. **paþas,** in which the stem-vowel **a** is due to retraction (§§ 27, 29). Examples of analogy in accidence are to be found in the tendencies, beginning in the Old English period but greatly increased since then, for strong verbs to become weak and for nouns to pass from other declensions into the **a**-declension.

CHAPTER I

VOWELS OF STRONGLY STRESSED SYLLABLES

17. The sound-changes described in §§ 18-21 took place in Common Germanic, and their effects are therefore to be seen in other Germanic languages as well as in Old English. The other sound-changes described in this chapter took place in Anglo-Frisian or in Old English. Most of them took place before the date of the earliest surviving Old English texts, and the vowels or consonants causing some sound-changes have themselves undergone change or have disappeared before this date. It is, however, often possible to reconstruct the earlier form by comparing cognate words in other languages.

GERMANIC CHANGES

18. Before a nasal followed by another consonant **e** was raised to **i**. Hence in class III of strong verbs **bindan,** *to bind;* **drincan,** *to drink,* occur beside **bregdan,** *to brandish;* **helpan,** *to help.* Cf. also OE. **wind,** *wind,* cognate with Latin **ventus.**

19. The same change of **e** to **i** took place if **i** or **j** occurred in the next syllable. The **i** or **j** which caused the change generally later disappeared or was weakened to **e**. Hence 2, 3 sing. pres. ind. **bir(e)st, bir(e)þ; hilpst, hilpþ** beside **beran,** *to carry;* **helpan,** *to help.*

20. When followed in Germanic by **a, ō,** or **ǣ** in the next syllable, (*a*) **u** became **o**, and (*b*) **i** often became **e**, unless a nasal followed by another consonant or an **i** or a **j** came between. Hence in class III of strong verbs we have **holpen** pp. of **helpan,** *to help,* beside **bunden** pp. of **bindan,** *to bind,* since in Germanic the vowel of the participial ending was **a,** which became **e** in Old English. Cf. also **wer,** *man,* from Gmc. * **weraz,** cognate with Latin **vir.**

21. After the change described in § 18, **n** disappeared with compensatory lengthening of the preceding vowel when it was immediately followed by **h** (§ 78). The long vowels resulting from this change were at first nasalized, and the

13

nasalized **ā** underwent the further change to **ō** in primitive Old English (see § 23 for the similar change of **ā** to **ō** before a nasal). Examples are : **þōhte** (from * **þanhta**) pret. of **þencan**, *to think;* **þūhte** (from * **þunhta**) pret. of **þyncan**, *to seem;* **fōn** (from * **fōhan**, earlier * **fanhan**), to *seize* (cf. Gothic **fāhan**).

THE INFLUENCE OF NASAL CONSONANTS

22. Loss of nasal with compensatory lengthening of the preceding vowel and rounding of **a** to **o**, similar to that described in § 21, took place in Anglo-Frisian in groups consisting of vowel + nasal + a voiceless fricative other than **h**, i.e. [f], [s], [θ]. Hence **cūþe** (from * **kunþ-**) pret. of **cunnan**, *to know;* **tōþ**, *tooth* (from * **tanþ-**) ; **gōs**, *goose* (from * **gans-**) ; **sōfte**, *softly* (cf. OHG. **samfto**).

23. WGmc. **ā** before a nasal consonant became rounded in Old English and fell in with **ō**, from WGmc. **ō**. Hence in class IV of strong verbs **cōmon**, **nōmon**, pret. of **cuman**, *to come*, **niman**, *to take*, occur beside **bǣron**, pret. of **beran**, *to carry*, where WGmc. **ā** has been fronted to **ǣ** (§ 28).

24. WGmc. **a** before a nasal consonant became slightly rounded in Old English to a vowel between **a** and **o** in sound. In the earliest Old English manuscripts the usual spelling is **a**; in early West Saxon **o** is the more common; in late West Saxon **a** again becomes more common than **o**. Examples are **mann, monn**, *man;* **land, lond**, *land.*

25. WGmc. **e** was raised in Old English to **i** before **m**. Hence **niman**, *to take*, belongs to the same class of strong verbs as **beran**, *to carry.*

26. WGmc. **o** was raised in Old English to **u** before nasals, as in **numen**, pp. of **niman**, *to take*, beside **boren**, pp. of **beran**, *to carry.*

FRONTING OF å AND RETRACTION OF ǣ

27. Gmc. **a,** when not rounded before a nasal (§ 24), was fronted to **æ** in Old English. Examples are **dæg**, *day* (cf. Gothic **dags**) ; **fæger**, *fair* (cf. Gothic **fagrs**).

This **æ** was generally retracted to **a** in the following conditions :

(*a*) in an open syllable when a back vowel followed in the next syllable, as in nom. pl. **dagas, fatu** beside nom. sing. **dæg**, *day*; **fæt**, *vessel ;*

(*b*) before **w** if **i** did not follow, as in **clawe,** gen. and dat. sing. of **clēa,** *claw* (cf. § 62) ;

(*c*) in Anglian before l + consonant, as in Ang. **ald,** *old;* **cald,** *cold.*

28. WGmc. **ā,** which developed by an independent change from Gmc. **ǣ,** was fronted to **ǣ** in Old English, except when the **ā** had already been rounded before a nasal (§ 23). Examples are: **sǣd,** *seed* (cf. OHG. **sāt**); **bǣdon** pret. pl. of **biddan,** *to pray.*

The **ǣ** was generally retracted to **ā** in open syllables when a back vowel followed in the next syllable provided that certain consonants (especially **g, w** and **r**) intervened. Hence **sāwon, lāgon,** pret. of **sēon,** *to see,* **licgan,** *to lie ;* **māgas,** pl. of **mǣg,** *kinsman.*

29. Analogy often interfered with the regular operation of retraction of both **æ** and **ǣ,** and we therefore find forms like **paþes,** gen. sing. of **pæþ,** *path;* **paþe,** dat. sing. (beside **pæþes, pæþe**) on the analogy of plural forms like **paþas.** Similarly we find **wǣron,** *were,* **lǣgon,** *lay,* on the analogy of preterites like **sǣton,** *sat,* or of subjunctive forms like **wǣren, lǣgen.**

30. In Kentish and South Mercian the **æ** that resulted from fronting underwent the further change to **e,** and in most non-West Saxon dialects the **ǣ** that resulted from fronting was raised to **ē** before the earliest written records.

FRACTURE

31. Fracture, or breaking, is the name given to the diphthongization of front vowels before certain back consonants. The change was caused by the movement of the tongue from the front to the back position without interruption of the current of air passing through the mouth. The result was that a back vowel-glide was developed between the front vowel and the back consonant, and this glide then combined with the preceding vowel to form a diphthong. The consonant which caused fracture most readily was **h,** but l and r also caused the change when they were followed by another consonant.

32. The changes in detail were :

(*a*) **æ** became **ea** before **h** or **h** + consonant, before **r** + consonant, and (in West Saxon) before l + consonant. Hence in class III of strong verbs **feohtan**, *to fight*, **weorpan**, *to throw*, **helpan**, *to help*, have preterites **feaht**, **wearp**, **healp**, whereas **bregdan**, *to brandish*, has pret. **brægd**; cf. also **sealde**, pret. of **sellan**, *to give*.

(b) e becomes **eo** before **h** or **h** + consonant, before **r** + consonant, and before **lh** and **lc**. Hence in strong verbs of class III **feohtan**, *to fight;* **beorgan**, *to protect;* **feolan**, *to penetrate* (from * **feolhan**, see §§ 64(c), 98) ; **āseolcan**, *to become sluggish*, occur beside **helpan**, *to help;* **bregdan**, *to brandish*.

(c) **i** became **io** (which later usually became **eo** in West Saxon) before **h** or **h** + consonant and before **r** + consonant. Examples are : **liornian, leornian**, *to learn;* **tiohhian, teohhian**, *to think*.

(d) Long vowels were broken only before **h**: **æ**, **ē**, **ī** became **ēa**, **ēo**, **īo** (later **ēo**) respectively. At the time of fracture **æ** occurred only in West Saxon and closely neighbouring dialects, while **ē** was rare in West Saxon though it was common elsewhere (§ 30). Examples are : **nēah**, *near;* **tēon**, *to accuse* (earlier * **tīhan**).

33. Anglian carried out fracture less often than West Saxon. In Anglian, **a** occurs in place of WS. **ea** before **l** + consonant (§ 27(c)) and sometimes before **r** + consonant, especially in the neighbourhood of labials, as in Ang. **ald**, *old;* **barn** beside **bearn**, *child*.

34. It is probable that fracture was later than the fronting of **a** (§ 27), since it is phonetically more likely for a front vowel **æ** than for a back vowel **a** to be affected by fracture (§ 31). It is probable that fracture was earlier than retraction of **æ** to **a** (§ 27) since fracture took place in such forms as **slēan**, *to strike* (from * **sleahan**, cf. Gothic **slahan**).

35. A few Old English words have an unfractured vowel before **r** + consonant ; examples are **irnan**, *to run*, and its pret. **arn; berstan**, *to burst*, and its pret. **bærst**. Fracture has not taken place in these forms, because at the date of fracture **r** preceded the vowel, and metathesis has later taken place (§ 91).

FRONT DIPHTHONGIZATION

36. The voiceless velar plosive consonant **c** and the voiced velar fricative **g** were fronted in primitive Old English when immediately followed by front vowels (§ 83), and **c** in the group **sc** was fronted whatever the quality of the following vowel. In West Saxon the front **c** and **g** and **sc** then caused diphthongization of the following front vowels **e**, **æ**, and **ǣ**, to **ie**, **ea** and **ēa** respectively. The off-glide from the consonant combined with the following vowel to form first a rising diphthong and then, the former glide element taking the stress, a falling diphthong. Examples are **gieldan**, *to pay* (cf. OS. **geldan**); **giefan**, *to give* (cf. ON. **gefa**), pret. sing. **geaf**, pret. pl. **gēafon**; **ciele**, *cold;* **scieran**, *to cut.*

37. Front diphthongization was later than fracture (§ 31), as is suggested by such forms as **ceorfan**, *to cut;* **georn**, *eager.* The vowel in each word was **e** in Germanic. If front diphthongization had preceded fracture in these words, the **e** would have given **ie**.

38. The spelling **g** was often used in Old English to represent [j], from Gmc. **j**, as in **geong** beside **iung**, *young* (cf. Gothic **juggs**) ; **gēar**, *year* (cf. German **Jahr**). After **g** of this origin and after **sc**, we often find the digraph **eo** in Old English, even when the stem-vowel was originally back, as in **sceort**, *short;* **sceolde**, *should;* **geoc**, *yoke;* **geong**, *young.* It is not certain whether these spellings represented true diphthongs in Old English or whether the front vowel was inserted merely as a spelling device to indicate the front quality of the preceding consonant. The later development generally supports the view that no diphthongization took place (cf. MnE. *short, should, yoke, young*), but it may be that the Modern English forms are from non-West-Saxon dialects in which as a rule front diphthongization did not take place.

FRONT MUTATION

39. Front mutation, or **i/j**-mutation, is the name given to the modification of a vowel or diphthong by an **i**, **ī** or **j** in the following syllable. By the time of the surviving Old English texts the **ī** or **j** which caused the change had generally either disappeared or been weakened to **e**, but the existence of the **ī** or **j** in primitive Old English can be deduced from the influence on the preceding vowel and by comparison with cognate languages. Front mutation is one of the most important Old English sound-changes, and most vowels were affected by it. The effect of the change was to cause the vowel affected to approach **i** in its place of formation. Hence back vowels were raised and front open vowels became more close.

40. The changes due to front mutation are as follows :

a became **æ** as in Ang. **ældra** (comp. of **ald,** *old*) ; **færeþ** (3 sing. pres. ind. of **faran,** *to go*).

æ, which resulted from fronting (§ 27), usually became **e,** but **æ** is sometimes found before consonant groups. Examples are : **efnan** beside **æfnan,** *to perform;* **settan,** *to set,* from * **sættjan,** earlier * **satjan** (cf. Gothic **satjan**) ; **here,** *army,* from * **hæri** (cf. Gothic **harjis**).

a or **o** before a nasal (§ 24) usually became **e,** though **æ** is found in some south-eastern dialects, as in **fremman,** beside **fræmman,** *to perform,* from * **framjan** (cf. **fram,** *bold*)*;* **menn** (dat. sing. and nom. acc. pl. of **mann, monn,** *man*).

o became **e** through the stage **œ** as in **dehter,** dat. sing. of **dohtor,** *daughter.*

u became **y** as in **cymest, cymeþ** (2, 3 sing. pres. ind. of **cuman,** *to come;* **þyncan,** *to seem,* from * **þunkjan**) (cf. pret. **þūhte** from * **þunht-**).

ā became **ǣ** as in **hǣlan,** *to heal* (cf. **hāl,** *whole*) ; **gǣst, gǣþ** (2, 3 sing. pres. ind. of **gān,** *to go*).

ō became **ē** through the stage **œ̄** as in **dēman,** *to judge,* from * **dōmjan** (cf. **dōm,** *judgement*) ; **sēcan,** *to seek* (cf. pret. **sōhte**).   The stage **œ̄** is sometimes kept in Anglian.

ū became **ȳ** as in **brȳcþ** (3 sing. pres. ind. of **brūcan,** *to enjoy*)*;* **fȳsan,** *to send forth* (cf. **fūs,** *eager*).

io or **eo** became **ie,** later **i** or **y,** in West Saxon but remained in non-West Saxon, as in WS. **fieht** (3 sing. pres. ind. of **feohtan,** *to fight*); **āfierran, āfirran, āfyrran,** *to remove* (cf. **feorr,** *far*); WS. **ierre,** Ang. **iorre, eorre,** *angry.*

īo or **ēo** became **īe,** later **ī** or **ȳ,** in West Saxon but remained in non-West Saxon, as in WS. **flīehþ** (3 sing. pres. ind. of **flēon**) ; WS. **strīenan, strīnan, strȳnan,** beside Ang. **strēonan,** *to acquire* (cf. **gestrēon,** *property*).

ea became **ie,** later **i** or **y,** in West Saxon, **e** in non-West Saxon, as in WS. **hliehhan, hlihhan,** *to laugh* (cf. Gothic **hlahjan**) ; WS. **ieldra,** Kt. **eldra,** comp. of **eald,** *old* (Ang. **ældra** is from **ald;** see § 33).

ēa became **īe,** later **ī** or **ȳ,** in West Saxon, **ē** in non-West Saxon, as in WS. **hīeran, hīran,** Ang. **hēran,** *to hear.*

41. The vowels **i, ī, ē, ǣ** are unaffected by front mutation in all dialects, and **io, īo** are unaffected in non-West Saxon. The vowel **e** had already become **i** before **i** or **j** in Gmc. (§ 19).

The mutation of **a** or **o**, except before nasals, is rare, because at the date of front mutation these vowels did not normally occur in words in which **ĭ** or **j** stood in the next syllable (§§ 20, 27). When one of these vowels did occur before **ĭ** or **j** at the time of front mutation it was generally as the result of analogy. Examples are :

(*a*) In the 2, 3 sing. pres. ind. of the verb **faran**, WGmc. * **faris**, * **fariþ** would regularly give * **færis(t)**, * **færiþ** as the result of fronting, and these would become * **fer(e)st**, ***fer(e)þ** by front mutation followed by syncope or weakening of the unaccented **i** to **e** (§ 72). But after the time of fronting the **æ** was replaced by **a** on the analogy of such forms as **faran** inf. This analogical **a** was then mutated to **æ**, giving the forms which occur, **fær(e)st**, **fær(e)þ**.

(*b*) **dehter** (dat. sing. of **dohtor**, *daughter*) is from * **dohtri**, in which **o** from other cases of the noun has replaced the phonologically regular **u** in * **duhtri**, which would have given * **dyhter** in Old English.

42. In some pairs of words there is a variation between **o** and **y**, as in **fox**, *fox*, beside **fyxen**, *vixen;* **gold**, *gold*, beside **gylden**, *golden;* **coss**, *a kiss*, beside **cyssan**, *to kiss*. The reason for the variation is that both **o** and **y** go back to earlier **u**. The forms **fox**, **gold** and **coss** earlier had endings containing **a**, which caused the stem-vowel **u** to become **o** (§ 20) ; **fyxen**, **gylden** and **cyssan** had **ĭ** or **j** in the second syllable with the result that the stem-vowel **u** underwent front mutation to **y**.

43. Verbs belonging to the second weak class do not show front mutation of the stem-vowel, because the **i** of the ending arose after the time of this change. The ending in Germanic was * **-ōjan**. The **j** mutated the immediately preceding vowel to **ē**, and the eudign *-**ējan**, being weakly stressed, was then reduced to **-ian**.

44. Front mutation is later than fracture (§ 31), as is shown by such forms as WS. **ieldra** (comp. of **eald**, *old*) or **wiext** (3 sing. pres. ind. of **weaxan**, *to grow*, from * **weahsan**). The development of the stem vowel has been **a** > **æ** > **ea** > **ie;** if front mutation had been earlier than fracture the development would have been **a** > **æ** > **e** > (**eo**). Front mutation is later than front diphthongization (§ 36), as is shown by such forms as late WS. **cȳse**, *cheese*, from * **cāsi-**, from Latin **cāseus**. The development of the stem vowel has been ā > ǣ > ēa > īe > ȳ; if front mutation had been earlier than front diphthongization the development would have been ā > ǣ > ēa.

BACK MUTATION

45. Short front vowels (**i, e** or **æ**) were often diphthongized to **io, eo, ea,** in Old English when a back vowel (**u, o** or **a**) occurred in the following syllable. This change is similar to fracture but took place some time later. As a rule back mutation took place only before single consonants, though there are occasional exceptions, such as **siondon,** *are* ; **seoþþan,** *afterwards*. The change was carried out more fully in non-West Saxon than in West Saxon, where it was limited to the back mutation of **i** when followed by **u, o** or **a,** and to the back mutation of **e** when followed by **u,** and generally took place only before labial and liquid consonants. In Kentish the change took place before all single consonants ; in Anglian it is not normally found before the back consonants **c, g, h.** The **u** which caused mutation was generally lowered to **o** or syncopated before the date of most of the written texts. Regular West Saxon examples are :

(*a*) **e** became **eo** before **u,** as in **heofun, heofon,** *heaven;* **heolstor** (earlier **helustr**), *darkness;* **heorot,** *hart*.

(*b*) **i** became **io** (later **eo**) (i) before **u,** as in **siolufr, siolfor,** *silver;* **cliopude, cliopode,** pret. of **clipian,** *to call;* (ii) before **a,** as in **hiora, heora** gen. pl. *their;* **liofas(t), liofaþ** (2, 3 sing. pres. ind. of **libban,** *to live*).

46. The effects of back mutation are often removed by analogy, especially in West Saxon. For example, WS. pl. **clifu, scipu,** beside Ang. **cliofu, sciopu,** are due to the influence of the sing. **clif,** *cliff,* and **scip,** *ship*.

47. The back mutation of **æ** to **ea** generally took place only in Mercian, in which dialect **æ** had either never been retracted or had been fronted again. Examples are : Mercian **featu** pl. *vessels;* **fearan,** *to go*. In other dialects **æ,** when followed by a back vowel in the next syllable, was retracted before the date of back mutation. Only a few words in West Saxon show the back mutation of **æ** to **ea,** the most common of which is **ealu,** *ale*.

48. When followed by a back vowel in the next syllable and also preceded by **w**, the vowels **i**, **e**, often became **u**, **o**, as in **wudu**, *wood* (cf. ON. **viðr**) ; **swutol**, *evident;* **wuta**, *wise man ;* **woruld**, *world;* **swostor**, *sister.*

THE INFLUENCE OF PALATAL CONSONANTS

49. In all the Old English dialects the palatal consonants **c**, **g** and **sc** exerted an influence on following vowels and diphthongs, and **c**, **g** and **h** exerted an influence on preceding vowels and diphthongs. This influence, often described as smoothing, generally took the form of the monophthongization of diphthongs or the unrounding of **y**. Details of the changes follow.

50. The diphthongs **eo** and **io**, which had arisen by fracture of **e** and **i** before **hs** (later spelt **x**) and **ht** (§ 32) became **ie** in early West Saxon when not followed by a back vowel in the next syllable ; later this **ie** became **y** or **i**. Regular forms are **siex, six, syx**, *six;* **cniht**, *youth*, beside pl. **cneohtas; feohtan**, *to fight*. Then levelling out took place in both directions, resulting in forms like **cneoht**, sing., **cnihtas**, pl. and **gefeoht**, sb. *fight.*

51. Early WS. **ĭe**, of whatever origin, became **y̆** or **ĭ** in late West Saxon. The **ĭ** is especially common in the neighbourhood of **c**, **g**, **h** or **sc**, but is sometimes found in other positions. Examples are **giefan, gyfan, gifan**, *to give;* **hieran, hȳran, hiran**, *to hear;* **ieldra, yldra**, *older.*

52. Before palatal **c**, **g**, **h** or **n**, early OE. **y̆** often became **ĭ** in late Old English. Examples are **cynn, cinn**, *race;* **dryhten, drihten**, *lord.*

53. In late West Saxon, **ĕa** often became **ĕ** when preceded by **c**, **g** or **sc** or when followed by **c**, **g** or **h**, as in **cerf** beside **cearf**, pret. of **ceorfan**, *to cut;* **gēr** beside **gēar**, *year;* **scĕp**, beside **scĕap**, *sheep;* **bĕcen** beside **bĕacen**, *beacon;* **bēg** beside **bēag**, *ring;* **ehta** beside **eahta**, *eight.*

54. In Anglian the diphthongs **ĕa, ĕo, ĭo** were smoothed to **ǣ, ĕ** and **ĭ** before **c**, **g**, **h**, whether standing alone or preceded by a liquid ; **ǣ** of this origin generally later became **ē**, and **æ** often became **e**, especially before a liquid + **c**, **g** or **h**. Examples are Ang. **færh**, *pig;* **æge, ēge**, *eye;* **werc**, *work;* **sēc**, *sick;* **gesihð**, *sight;* **wĭh**, *idol;* beside early West Saxon **fearh, ēage, weorc, sēoc, gesiehð, wēoh.**

THE INFLUENCE OF LABIAL CONSONANTS

55. A few Old English words have **u** where, according to § 20, we should expect **o**. The **u** is found especially before and after labials, as in **full**, *full;* **fugol**, *bird;* **lufian**, *to love;* **wulf**, *wolf.*

56. Before antevocalic **w** the front vowel **e** (whether derived from Gmc. **e** or resulting from front mutation) was diphthongized to **eo**, as in **treowes** gen. sing. of **trēo**, *tree;* **eowestre**, *sheepfold* (cf. Gothic **awistr**) ; **meowle**, *maiden* (cf. Gothic **mawilō**). The **ēo** in **trēo** had a different origin (§ 62).

57. Before **w** belonging to the same syllable, **ǣ** often became **ēa**, and **ē** became **ēo**, as in **brēaw** beside **brǣw**, *eyelid;* **spēowð**, **flēowð** (3 sing. pres. ind. of **spōwan**, *to succeed* and **flōwan**, *to flow*).

58. A preceding **w** often caused rounding of **i**. Rounding is especially common when the **w** disappeared as the result of contraction with the negative particle (§ 94). Examples are **hwylc**, *which;* **wyllan**, *to be willing;* **nyllan**, *to be unwilling;* **nyste** pret., *did not know.*

59. In late West Saxon the group **weo** of whatever origin became **wu**, less often **wo**, and the group **wio** (earlier **wi**) became **wu**. Examples are : **swurd**, *sword*, earlier **sweord; swustor**, *sister*, earlier **sweostor; cwucu**, *alive*, from **cwicu** probably through an intermediate stage with **io** by back mutation (§ 45) ; **wuht**, *thing*, from **wiht**, probably through an intermediate stage with **io** by fracture (§ 32).

60. The group **wyr** became **wur** in late West Saxon, as in **wurm** from older **wyrm**, *serpent;* **wursa** from older **wyrsa**, *worse.*

CONTRACTION

61. As a result of the loss of medial **w, j** and **h** (§§ 93, 95, 98), two vowels often came to stand together. When this happened the first vowel, which generally bore the stronger stress, either absorbed the following vowel or combined with it to form a diphthong. It is convenient to distinguish between contraction resulting from loss of **w** on the one hand and that resulting from loss of **j** or **h** on the other.

62. **w** disappeared before **u** or **i**. When the following vowel was **u**, after the loss of the **w** it combined with a preceding **a, e** or **i** to form a diphthong **au, eu, iu**. These diphthongs gave OE. **ēa, ēo, īo**. Examples are **clēa,** *claw,* earlier **clawu,** cf. dat. sing. **clawe; trēo,** from * **trewu,** nom. pl. of **trēo,** *tree.* When the following vowel was **i,** after the loss of the **w** it caused front mutation of a preceding back vowel and was then absorbed by the resulting front vowel, as in **sǣ,** *sea,* earlier * **sāwi-,** Gmc. * **saiwiz.**

63. When contraction was due to the loss of intervocalic **j** or **h** the following rules can be given :

(*a*) A front vowel **ǣ, ě, ī** absorbed a following front vowel, but formed a diphthong with a following back vowel, as in Ang. **sīþ,** *sees,* earlier * **sihiþ;** OE. **fēond,** *enemy,* cf. Gothic **fijands.** On West Saxon forms like **siehþ** see § 98.

(*b*) A back vowel **ā, ǒ, ǔ** absorbed any following vowel, with the exception that **ū** generally remained uncontracted when followed by **a.** Examples are **fōn,** *to seize,* earlier * **fōhan;** beside **scū(w)a,** *shadow.*

(*c*) A diphthong absorbed any following vowel, as in **sēon,** *to see,* earlier * **seohan; hēas,** gen. sing. masculine of **hēah,** *high.*

64. Short vowels were lengthened under certain conditions :

(*a*) In Gmc. short vowels were lengthened in compensation for the loss of a nasal before the fricative **h** (§ 21), and in primitive Old English they were lengthened in compensation for the loss of a nasal before other voiceless fricatives (§ 22).

(*b*) Final short vowels were lengthened in monosyllables when they had strong sentence-stress, as in **hwā,** *who;* **hē,** *he.*

(*c*) When **h** disappeared between vowels (§ 98), a preceding short vowel was lengthened, as in **slēan,** *to strike* (from * **sleahan,** cf. Gothic **slahan**). When **h** disappeared between a liquid and a vowel, lengthening of the stem-vowel may have taken place, but the later development of place-names such as *Wales, Sale* and *Hale* suggests that the vowel remained short.

(*d*) When **g** disappeared before **d** or **n** (§ 99) a preceding short vowel was lengthened, as in **sǣde** beside **sægde** pret. of **secgan,** *to say;* **frīnan** beside **frignan,** *to ask.*

(*e*) Front **g** often disappeared after **i** in late Old English with compensatory lengthening of the vowel if this were short.

The change took place earliest in the group -igi-, as in **il**
beside **igil,** *hedgehog;* **lïþ** 3 sing. pres. ind. of **licgan,** *to lie.*
It took place most readily in lightly stressed syllables, where
ī was later shortened again, as in **dysi,** *foolish;* **ǣni,** *any.*

(*f*) In late Old English short vowels were often lengthened
before a liquid or nasal followed by a voiced consonant,
(i.e. before **ld, mb, nd, ng, rd, rl, rn**). Lengthening before **r +**
consonant was less frequent and less lasting in its effects than
before the other groups, and no lengthening took place when
the consonant group was immediately followed by another
consonant. Examples are **húnd** beside **hundred,** *hundred;*
cïld, *child,* beside **cïldru** pl. (the variation in length has been
preserved in MnE. *child* beside *children*). Lengthening
did not normally take place in lightly stressed words such as
wolde, *would;* **under,** *under;* **and,** *and.*

SHORTENING OF VOWELS

65. There has been a tendency to shorten long vowels
under varying conditions at many periods during the history
of the English language. It is probable that long vowels
were shortened in the Old English period under the following
conditions :

(*a*) Before three consonants, as in **godspell,** *gospel;*
brǣmblas, pl. *brambles.* No shortening took place in Old
English before **st** followed by a liquid, as in **wrǣstlian,** *to
wrestle.*

(*b*) Before two consonants in words of more than two
syllables, as in **bledsian,** *to bless* (from * **blōðisōjan**).

(*c*) Before double consonants, as in **lǣssa,** *less;* **ænne** acc.,
one; **wimman,** *woman;* **siððan,** *afterwards.*

66. Analogy often prevented shortening in forms like
clǣnsian, *to cleanse* (cf. **clǣne,** *clean*); **mētte** pret. of **mētan,**
to meet; **fēdde** pret. of **fēdan,** *to feed.* No shortening took
place in compound words which were still regarded as such.
For example, MnE. *homestead* is from OE. **hám-stede,** where
the influence of **hám,** *home,* has preserved the long vowel ;
the place-name *Hampstead* is from a form in which shortening
of **á** has taken place before a group of three consonants.

67. It is often difficult to fix even the approximate
date of shortening, but it is clear that shortening of **ī** preceded
back mutation in **seoððan** (§ 45) ; on the other hand, in
brǣmblas shortening is later than syncope of **i** (§ 72).

CHAPTER II

VOWELS OF LIGHTLY STRESSED SYLLABLES

FINAL VOWELS

68. Except after short monosyllables, prim. OE. i and ī disappeared finally, as in **giest**, *stranger;* **fēt**, *feet.* It is clear from these examples that the loss of final i was later than front mutation. After short monosyllables i was weakened to **e**, as in **wine**, *friend.*

69. Prim. OE. ō became **u.** This is the origin of the final **-u** in the nom. sing. of ō-stem nouns (§ 109), the nom. acc. pl. of neuter **a**-stems (§ 108), and the 1 sing. pres. ind. of verbs in Anglian (§ 157). This **-u**, like final -u of other origins, disappeared after long monosyllables and after dissyllabic stems of which the first syllable was short; in other conditions final unaccented **-u** remained. Examples are **hand**, *hand* (cf. Gothic **handus**), beside **sunu**, *son;* nom. acc. pl. **werod**, *troops*, beside **hĕafdu**, *heads*.

Note 1.—Analogy often led to the loss of -u after dissyllabic stems even when the first syllable was long, and in the nom. sing. of dissyllabic feminine nouns forms without -u are usual, whatever the length of the first syllable, as **sāwol**, *soul.*

Note 2.—In later Old English, -u was weakened to -o or **-a** as in **suno**, **suna** beside **sunu**, *son*.

MEDIAL VOWELS

70. The vowels ī and i fell together as **i**, which remained in the earliest texts but later usually became **e**, except when it was syncopated (§ 72). Examples are early OE. **birist**, **biriþ**, later **birest**, **bireþ**, 2, 3 sing. pres. ind. of **beran**, *to carry;* **gylden**, *golden* (cf. Gothic **gulþeins**). Before a palatal consonant i remained, as in **bysig**, *busy;* **Englisc**, *English.*

71. Gmc. **a** remained before n belonging to the same syllable, as in the infinitive ending **-an**, but became **e**, through the intermediate stage **æ**, in other positions, as in **dæges**, older **dægæs**, gen. sing. of **dæg**, *day.* Before g the **e** underwent the further change to **i**, as in **hunig** beside **huneg**, *honey;* **manig** beside **maneg**, *many* (cf. Gothic **manags**). The change of **e** to **i**

before g was later than front mutation, as is shown by the
absence of front mutation in **hunig** and **manig.** The OE.
suffix -ig has two origins : Gmc. -ig- (cf. Gothic **mahteigs,**
mighty), and Gmc. -ag- (cf. Gothic **manags,** *many*). The first
of these suffixes caused front mutation ; the second did not.
Hence we have in Old English **bysig,** *busy,* beside **manig,** *many.*
On the -en in the pp. of strong verbs, see § 162.

72. Medial unaccented vowels were syncopated in Old
English after a long syllable provided that they were followed
by a single consonant, as in **hālgum,** dat. pl. of **hālig,** *holy;*
dēmde, pret. sing. of **dēman,** *to judge.* They remained after
a short syllable, as in **heofones,** gen. sing. of **heofon,** *heaven;*
nerede, pret. sing. of **nerian,** *to save.* They usually also remained if preceded or followed by a consonant group since
their loss in such positions would have left a group of consonants difficult to pronounce. Examples are **cyninges,** gen. sing.
of **cyning,** *king;* **hyngrede,** pret. sing. of **hyngran,** *to be hungry.*

73. Medial o often became e by dissimilation when the
following syllable contained one of the back vowels **u, o,** or
a, as in **heofenas** beside **heofonas,** pl. of **heofon,** *heaven;* **clipedon**
beside **clipodon,** pret. pl. of **clipian,** *to call.*

74. When a liquid or nasal preceded by another consonant
came to stand finally as the result of the loss of a following
vowel, a new vowel was developed before the liquid or nasal
in Old English. This vowel was usually **e** after a front stem-
vowel and **u** or **o** after a back stem-vowel. Examples are
æcer, *field* (cf. Gothic **akrs**); **fugol,** *bird* (cf. Gothic **fugls**).

75. A vowel was often developed between **r** or **l** and **c, g,**
or **h.** The quality of the vowel thus developed depended
upon the quality of the preceeding stem-vowel. After front
vowels it was usually **i;** after back vowels it was **u** or **o.**
Examples are: nom. sing. **bur(u)g, bur(u)h,** *city;* dat. sing.
byr(i)g; fyl(i)gan, *to follow;* **woruhte, worohte** beside **worhte,**
pret. sing. of **wyrcan,** *to work.*

76. A similar vowel was often developed between **r, l,**
d, or **t** and **w.** The vowel thus developed was usually **u** or
o, but sometimes **e** is found. Examples are gen. dat. sing.
beaduwe, beadowe beside **beadwe,** cf. nom. sing. **beadu,** *battle;*
frætuwe, frætewe beside **frætwe,** *trappings.*

CHAPTER III

CONSONANTS

GERMANIC CHANGES

77. The medial voiceless fricatives [f], [s], [θ], and [x] became voiced in Germanic to [ƀ], [z], [ð], and [γ] when they occurred between voiced sounds unless they were immediately preceded by the chief stress of the word. This change, generally known as Verner's Law, has had an effect on a large number of Old English words, but later changes have often obscured its results. It is clear that at the time of the change the chief stress in strong verbs was on the stem in the infinitive and the preterite singular but on the ending in the preterite plural and past participle. Hence the preterite plural and past participle show the effects of the change whereas the infinitive and the preterite singular do not. The regular alternation between voiceless and voiced fricatives has been obscured by such later developments as the changes of [z] to [r] (§ 79) and of [ð] to [d] (§ 80) in WGmc. and the voicing of [f], [s] and [θ] between voiced sounds (§ 84) and the loss of h between vowels (§ 98) in Old English. Examples are :

[f] > [ƀ] **geaf** pret. sing. of **giefan,** *to give,* beside pret. pl. **gēafon.** The spelling **f** represents [f] in **geaf** and [v] or [ƀ] in **gēafon** and **giefan** (§ 13(*a*)). The voiced fricative in **giefan** is due to the change described in § 84.

[s] > [z] **cēas** pret. sing of **cēosan,** *to choose,* beside pp. **gecoren** and **cyre,** sb. *choice.* The **r** is from earlier **z** (§ 79). The voicing of [s] to [z] in the infinitive **cēosan** (§ 84) is later than the WGmc. change of [z] to [r].

[θ] > [ð] **lāþ** pret. sing. of **līþan,** *to go,* beside pret. pl. **lidon** and **geliden,** with **d** from earlier [ð] (§ 80). The voicing of [θ] to [ð] in the infinitive **līþan** (§ 84) is later than the WGmc. change of [ð] to [d].

[x] > [γ] **sliehþ** 3 sing. pres. ind. of **slēan**, *to strike*, beside pret. pl. **slōgon** and pp. **geslǣgen**. The **h** in the infinitive has disappeared between vowels (§ 98). When the [x] and [γ] were preceded by **n**, the **n** disappeared before the [x] in prim. Gmc. (§§ 21, 78), but remained before [γ]. Hence we get **fēhþ**, 3 sing. pres. ind. of **fōn**, *to seize*, beside pret. pl. **fēngon** and pp. **gefangen**.

78. In Germanic after the operation of Verner's Law **n** disappeared before fricative **h** [x] with compensatory lengthening and nasalization of a preceding vowel. For the later development of the long nasalized vowels in Old English, see § 21. Examples of the change are : **pūhte**, *seemed* (the **n** is preserved in the infinitive **pyncan**, *to seem*, because there it is followed by **c** not **h**) ; **fōn**, *to seize*, from * **fōhan** (§ 98), earlier * **fanhan** (cf. the pp. **gefangen**).

WEST GERMANIC CHANGES

79. Gmc. [z], including the [z] which arose from [s] by Verner's Law (§ 77), became **r** medially and disappeared finally as in pp. **gecoren** beside infin. **cēosan**, *to choose;* **herian**, *to praise* (cf. Gothic **hazjan**); **dæg**, *day* (cf. Gothic **dags**).

80. Gmc. [ð], including the [ð] which arose from [θ] by Verner's Law (§ 77), became **d** as in pp. **geworden** beside infin. **weorþan**, *to become.*

81. All single medial consonants except **r** were doubled when immediately preceded by a short vowel and followed by **j**. In primitive Old English the **j** which had caused this change disappeared after a long stem but was vocalized to **i** after a short stem (§ 95). Hence, verbs of weak class I which have **r** as their medial consonant have the ending **-ian** whereas other verbs of this class have a double medial consonant and the ending **-an** (§ 193). Examples are **settan**, *to set* (from Gmc. * **satjan**) beside **nerian**, *to save* (cf. Gothic **nasjan**) ; **hliehhan**, *to laugh* (cf. Gothic **hlahjan**).

Note 1.—The double voiced fricative [vv] or [ƀƀ] which resulted from this change underwent the further change to the plosive [bb]. Since the voiced bi-labial or labio-dental fricative was generally spelt **f** in Old English (§ 13(*a*)), we have a variation in spelling between **f** and **bb**, as in **hebban**, *to raise*, beside pret. sing. **hōf**. On the development of **g** see § 83(*a*).

Note 2.—Before the operation of this change **j** disappeared before **i** and was vocalized to **i** when it occurred finally (§ 88). Hence doubling did not take place in the 2 and 3 sing. pres. ind. and in the imper. sing. of verbs, since the endings of the 2 and 3 sing. pres. ind. in Germanic were -**is**, -**iþ**, and the imper. sing. was normally the bare stem of the verb. Examples are OE. **legest, legeþ, lege** beside **lecgan**, *to lay;* **hefest, hefeþ, hefe** beside **hebban**, *to raise.*

82. The consonants **p, t, k,** and **h** were doubled in West Germanic when immediately followed by **l** or **r**. It is often difficult to distinguish between the forms resulting from this change and those resulting from a similar doubling which took place in Old English (§ 104), but the existence of forms with double consonants in Old Saxon and Old High German suggests the likelihood of some doubling by **l** and **r** in West Germanic. Analogy often led to the existence of pairs of forms, one with a single and the other with a double consonant. Thus we have regularly **biter**, *bitter*, beside analogical **bitter** with **tt** from the oblique cases; **æppel**, *apple*, with **pp** from such forms as gen. sing. **æpples**; ONhb. **tæhher**, *tear*, beside WS. **tēar**, from **teahur*, earlier **tahur*. In **æcer**, *field*, the single consonant of the nominative singular was levelled through the whole declension.

Fronting of Consonants

83. The consonants **c** and **g** were in Old English particularly liable to be modified by the influence of neighbouring sounds.

(*a*) The **gg** which resulted from the doubling influence of a following **j** in West Germanic (§ 81) was fronted by the influence of the same **j** to [dʒ], which was spelt **cg** in Old English, as in **secgan**, *to say;* **licgan**, *to lie.*

(*b*) Single **c** and **g** were fronted in Old English when they occurred next to front vowels. The front **g** which resulted from this change fell in with Gmc. [j] which was in consequence generally spelt **g**, less often **i**, in Old English. Examples of the fronting of **c** and **g** are **cēosan**, *to choose;* **giefan**, *to give.* Examples of the development of Gmc. [j] are **geong** beside **iung**, *young;* **geō** beside **iū**, *formerly.*

The fronting of **c** and **g** was earlier than front mutation (§ 39), and therefore **c** and **g** were not fronted before vowels which became front by front mutation, or secondary front vowels as they are sometimes called to distinguish them from primary front vowels which were already front in prim. Gmc. We may compare the Modern English pronunciation of *kin* (OE. **cynn**) with that of *chin* (OE. **cinn**).

(*c*) The **c** in the group **sc** was generally fronted, whatever the quality of the neighbouring vowels, and the group **sc** then came to be pronounced [ʃ].

Voicing

84. The voiceless fricatives [f], [s], and [θ] became voiced when they occurred medially between voiced sounds in simple words. The spelling was not affected in Old English (§ 13(*a*)), but evidence of the change is provided by the later development of words containing these sounds. Examples are **wulfas,** *wolves;* **nosu,** *nose;* **fæþm,** *embrace.* It is clear that this voicing was later than the West Germanic change of [z] to [r] (§ 79) since the [z] which resulted from it did not undergo the change to [r] : cf. inf. **cēosan,** *to choose* (with **s** pronounced [z]), pret. sing. **cēas** (with **s** in spelling and pronunciation), and pret. pl. **curon** (with **r** from [z] which had earlier arisen from [s] by Verner's Law (§ 77)).

Note.—In compound words the analogy of the simple word, in which the fricative was not medial, was generally enough to prevent voicing from taking place, as in **onfindan,** *to discover;* **gesittan,** *to sit.*

Unvoicing

85. The voiced fricatives [ð], [ɣ] became unvoiced when they occurred finally. The unvoicing of [ɣ] is recorded in spelling by the use of **h;** the unvoicing of [ð] is not recorded in spelling in Old English, since **f** was used to represent both the voiced and the unvoiced labial fricatives. Examples are pret. **geaf,** *gave;* **burh,** *city,* beside **burg; bēah,** *ring,* beside **bēag,** with **g** introduced by analogy from such forms as gen. sing. **bēages.** On unvoicing resulting from assimilation see § 90.

Vocalization

86. Between consonants **w** was vocalized to **o,** as in **gearone,** acc. sing. masculine, **gearore,** gen. sing. feminine beside **gearwes,** gen. sing. masculine of **gearu,** *ready.*

87. When **w** became final as a result of the loss of inflectional endings, it was vocalized to **u**. This **u** then had a threefold development :

(*a*) After a long syllable it disappeared, as in **snā,** *snow* (cf. Gothic **snáiws**), **gād,** *lack* (cf. Gothic **gáidw**).

(*b*) After a short syllable followed by a consonant it remained, as in **bearu,** *grove* (cf. nom. pl. **bearwas**).

(*c*) After a short syllable not followed by a consonant the **u** combined with the preceding vowel to form a diphthong, as in **trēo,** *tree* (from * **treu,** earlier * **trew-**).

Forms like **snāw, trēow** have **w** on the analogy of the oblique cases.

88. When **j** became final as a result of the loss of inflectional endings, it was vocalized to **-i,** later **-e,** as in **here,** *invading army.* (Cf. Gothic **harjis**.)

89. Palatal **g** often became **i** after vowels, and this **i** combined with the preceding vowel to form a diphthong, as in **dæi,** *day,* beside **dæg; wei,** *way,* beside **weg.** When the preceding vowel was **i,** the **-ig** became **ī** (§ 64(*e*)), which was shortened in an unaccented syllable, as in **æni,** *any,* beside **ænig.** The medial group **-igi-** became **īas** a result of the vocalization of the **g,** as in **īl,** beside **igil,** *hedgehog;* **līþ** beside **ligeþ** from * **ligiþ,** *lies.*

Assimilation

90. When two consonants came to stand together as the result of the loss of an unaccented vowel or the addition of an inflectional ending, there was a tendency for them to be assimilated to each other. This assimilation might be complete or partial, and it might affect either or both of the two adjacent consonants. It might affect the place of formation of a consonant or it might have the effect of voicing or unvoicing a consonant (cf. the pronunciation of **s** in MnE. *cats* with that in *dogs*).

Examples are :

tþ > tt: sitt, *he sits,* from **sit(e)þ.**
sþ > st: cīest, *he chooses,* from **cīes(e)þ.**
gþ > hþ: liehþ, *he tells lies,* from **līeg(e)þ.**

dþ > tt: bitt, *he prays,* from **bid(e)þ.** In this word both consonants have been affected by assimilation : the **d** has

become unvoiced because it was followed by a voiceless
consonant and the pre-dental consonant þ has become a post-
dental because it was preceded by a post-dental. The stages
were **biðeþ** > * **biðþ** > * **bitþ** > **bitt.**

ðd > dd: **cȳdde**, from **cȳðde**, pret. of **cȳðan**, *to make known*.
td > tt: **sette**, from * **set(e)de**, pret. of **settan**, *to set*.
fn > mn > mm: **efn, emn, emm**,·*even*.
fm > mm: **wimman**, from **wīfman**, *woman*.
sr > ss: **lǣssa**, from * **lǣs(i)ra**, *smaller*.
hr > rr: **hierra**, *higher*, from **hīehra**.

Metathesis

91. Metathesis is the transposition of two adjacent sounds.
By this change antevocalic **r** often became postvocalic, as in
hors, *horse* (cf. ON. **hross**); **gærs,** *grass* (cf. Gothic **gras**);
berstan, *to burst* (cf. ON. **bresta**). The lack of fracture in
gærs and **berstan** shows that in these words metathesis was
later than fracture.
92. Medial and final consonant groups sometimes underwent metathesis in late Old English. Double forms occur,
one with metathesis and the other without. Examples are :
sc > **cs** (written **x**), as in **āxian**, *to ask*, beside **āscian** (the
form with **x** has survived to the present day in some dialects).

sp > **ps**, as in **æps**, *aspen*, beside **æspe.**
ps > **sp**, as in **wæsp**, *wasp*, beside **wæps.**

Loss of Consonants

93. w disappeared before **u, ō,** and unaccented **i** (which
later became **e**), as in **sceadu**, *shadow*, from * **skadwu; clēa,**
claw, from **cla(w)u** (§ 62) ; **gierep**, *he prepares*, from * **gar(w)iþ;**
gierede, *he prepared*, from * **garwiða; cōmon** beside **cwōmon**,
pret. pl. of **cuman**, *to come*. The **w** was often restored on the
analogy of forms in which it was not followed by **u,** as in
clawu, with **w** from such forms as dat. sing. **clawe.**
94. w and **h** disappeared in the second element of compound
words and in many verbal forms when a verb beginning with
w or **h** was contracted with the negative prefix **ne,** as in
hlāford, *lord*, from **hlāf-weard; līcuma,** *body*, from **līc-hama;**
næs, *was not*, from **ne wæs; nāt,** *does not know*, from **ne wāt;**

nolde, *would not,* from **ne wolde; næfde,** *had not,* from **ne hæfde.**

95. Medial **j** disappeared after long syllables (i.e. syllables which contained a long vowel or which ended with a consonant group), as in **dēman,** *to judge* (cf. Gothic **dōmjan**). Since the West Germanic doubling of consonants by **j** (§ 81) caused a preceding short syllable to become long, the **j** causing the change has always disappeared. Intervocalic **j** disappeared even after short syllables, as in **fēond,** *enemy* (cf. Gothic **fijands**).

96. Nasal consonants disappeared before the voiceless fricatives **f, s,** and **þ,** with compensatory lengthening of the preceding vowel, as in **fīf,** *five* (cf. Gothic **fimf**); **ūs,** *us* (cf. Gothic **uns**); **tōþ,** *tooth* (from * **tanþ-;** for the rounding of the vowel see § 22).

97. When a word contained a group of three consonants the middle consonant often disappeared, as in **el(n)boga,** *elbow;* **fæs(t)nian,** *to fasten;* **sel(d)lic,** *strange.*

98. **h** disappeared between vowels or between a liquid consonant (**l** or **r**) and a vowel. When the preceding vowel was short, the loss of **h** between vowels caused compensatory lengthening of the stem-vowel, as in **slēan,** *to strike* (cf. Gothic **slahan;** § 64(*c*)).

Note.—In West Saxon, syncope of the unaccented vowel in the 2, 3 sing. pres. ind. took place earlier than the loss of intervocalic **h.** Hence **h** normally remains in forms like **siehst, siehþ,** 2, 3 sing. pres. ind. of **sēon,** *to see.*

99. **g** often disappeared before **d** or **n** with lengthening of the preceding vowel (§ 64(*d*)), as in **gefrūnon** beside **ge-frugnon,** pret. pl. of **gefrignan,** *to learn;* **sǣde** beside **sægde,** pret. sing. of **secgan,** *to say;* **pēnian,** *to serve,* beside **þegnian.**

100. In lightly stressed syllables **n** disappeared in the group **ng** when the stem of the word ended in **n,** as in **cyni(n)g,** *king;* **peni(n)g,** *penny.*

Simplification

101. Double consonants were simplified when immediately preceded or followed by another consonant, as in pret. **cyste** beside **cyssan,** *to kiss;* 3 sing. pres. ind. **bint,** *he binds,* from * **bintt,** earlier **bindeþ** (§ 90) ; pret. **sende,** *sent,* from * **send-de.**

102. Double consonants were often simplified when they occurred finally, as in **man(n)**, *man;* **eal(l)**, *all.* The group **cg**, representing front **gg**, was not simplified, since it had probably become an affricative consonant [dʒ] by the date of this change (§ 13(*e*)).

103. In late Old English double consonants were simplified in lightly stressed syllables, as in **forgiefen(n)es**, *forgiveness;* **bliccet(t)an**, *to glitter.*

Doubling of Consonants

104. The consonants **l** and **r** caused doubling of preceding consonants during the Old English period. This change was similar to the West Germanic doubling of consonants by **l** and **r** (§ 82), but it affected consonants (such as **d**) which were not affected by the earlier change, and it affected consonants which came to be immediately followed by **l** or **r** by reason of the syncope of unaccented vowels in Old English. Examples are **blæddre**, *bladder*, beside older **blædre**; **hwittra**, *whiter*, beside older **hwītra**; **miccles** besides older **micles**, gen. s.ng. of **micel**, *great.* For the shortening of long vowels in such words see § 65(*c*).

Minor Consonant Changes

105. In late Old English inflexional endings final **-m** often became **-n**. This process was carried much further in Middle English. Old English examples are dat. pl. **dagon, sunun** beside **dagum, sunum**, from **dæg**, *day*, **sunu**, *son.*

106. Germanic medial **lþ** became **ld**, as in **fealdan**, *to fold* (cf. Gothic **falþan**) ; **wilde**, *wild* (cf. Gothic **wilþeis**). The final **d** in words like **gold**, *gold* (cf. Gothic **gulþ**) and **beald**, *bold* (cf. Gothic **balþei**, *boldness*) is due to the analogy of the oblique cases.

107. Germanic **þl** appears as **dl** after long vowels in West Saxon, but remains in Anglian, as in WS. **nǣdl**, Ang. **nēþl**, *needle;* WS. **wǣdl**, Ang. **wēþl**, *poverty.*

CHAPTER IV

NOUNS

a- DECLENSION

108. Most masculine nouns are declined like **stān,** *stone.* Most neuter nouns are declined like **word,** *word,* if their stem-syllables are long (i.e. if they have a long vowel or if they end with a group of two consonants), but like **scip,** *ship,* if their stem-syllables are short (i.e. if they have a short vowel followed by a single consonant).

Sing.

Nom. Acc.	stān	word	scip
Gen.	stānes	wordes	scipes
Dat.	stāne	worde	scipe

Pl.

Nom. Acc.	stānas	word	scipu, -o
Gen.	stāna	worda	scipa
Dat.	stānum	wordum	scipum

It will be seen that the declension of neuter nouns differs from that of masculines only in the nominative and accusative plural.

Note 1.—Nouns whose stem-vowel was æ had **a** in the plural by retraction (§ 27). Examples are **dæg,** m. *day;* **fæt,** n. *vessel.*

Note 2.—In the oblique cases of nouns ending in **lh** or **rh** the **h** disappears (§ 98). Examples are **seolh,** m. *seal;* **feorh,** n. *life.*

Note 3.—In the oblique cases of dissyllabic nouns the lightly stressed vowel was generally syncopated after a long stem-syllable provided that it was followed by a single consonant (§ 72). Examples are **dryhten,** m. *lord,* gen. sing. **dryhtnes; hēafod,** n. *head,* gen. sing. **hēafdes;** beside **metod,** m. *creator,* gen. sing. **metodes; hlāford,** m. *lord,* gen. sing. **hlāfordes; wæter,** n. *water,* gen. sing. **wæteres.**

Note 4.—Some nouns have the ending -e (the survival of an earlier **j**) in the nom. and acc. sing., as **hierde,** m. *shepherd;* **bōcere,** m. *scribe.* Neuter nouns of this declension which have the ending -e in the nom. sing. have -u in the nom. and acc. pl., as **wīte,** *punishment;* **ǣrende,** *message.*

Note 5.—Nouns whose stems in prim. OE. ended in post-consonantal **w** have **w** in the oblique cases but -u in the nom. and acc. sing., as **bearu,** m. *grove;* **bealu,** n. *evil* (§ 87(*b*)). On nom. and acc. sing. **pēo(w),** m. *servant;* **trēo(w),** n. *tree,* besid gen. sing. **þeowes, treowes,** see §§ 56, 62, 87 (*c*).

Ō- DECLENSION

109. Most feminine nouns are declined like **ār,** *honour,*
if their stem-syllables are long, and like **giefu,** *gift,* if their
stem-syllables are short.

Sing.		
Nom.	**ār**	**giefu**
Acc.	**āre**	**giefe**
Gen.	**āre**	**giefe**
Dat.	**āre**	**giefe**
Pl.		
Nom.	**āra, -e**	**giefa, -e**
Acc.	**āra, -e**	**giefa, -e**
Gen.	**āra, ār(e)na**	**giefa, -ena**
Dat.	**ārum**	**giefum**

Note 1.—Nouns of this declension with dissyllabic stems in the nom.
sing. and with short second syllables generally show syncope of
the medial unaccented vowel in the oblique cases if the first syllable
is long but not if it is short (§ 72). Regular examples are **sāwle,**
acc. gen. dat. sing. of **sāwol,** *soul,* and **firene,** acc. gen. dat. sing. of
firen, *crime.* Dissyllabic nouns do not have the ending -**(e)na** in
the gen. pl.

Note 2.—On **beadu,** *battle,* and **mǣd,** *meadow,* beside acc. gen. dat. sing.
beadwe and **mǣdwe** see § 87.

Note 3.—On **clēa,** *claw,* beside acc. gen. dat. sing. **clawe** see § 62.

Note 4.—Two groups of abstract nouns were formed in Germanic from
adjectives by the addition of the suffixes -**iþō** and -**īn** respectively.
Both suffixes caused front mutation. Abstract nouns in -**iþō**
belonged to this declension in Germanic; those in -**īn** passed into
this declension when the suffix -**īn** was replaced by -**u** in Old English.
Early Old English examples are : nom. sing. **strengþu, -o,** *strength;*
menigu, -o, *multitude;* acc. gen. dat. sing. **strengþe, menige.**
In late Old English the -**u,** -**o** of the nom. sing. were extended to
the oblique cases and the nouns became indeclinable. Abstract
nouns in these groups do not as a rule occur in the plural.

Note 5.—Abstract nouns in -**ung** belong to this declension, but often
have -**a** in the oblique cases of the sing., as **wilnung,** *desire.*

i- DECLENSION

110. To this declension belongs a large number of abstract
nouns formed from the roots of verbs by the addition of the
suffix -**i** (later -**e**) or a dental suffix, as **cyre, cyst,** *choice* (cf.
cēosan, *to choose*). All nouns in -**scipe** and many names of
nations are masculine i-stems.

Sing.	Masculine	Neuter	Feminine
Nom. Acc.	wine, *friend*	spere, *spear*	dǣd, *deed*
Gen.	wines	speres	dǣde
Dat.	wine	spere	dǣde

Pl.			
Nom. Acc.	wine, -as	speru	dǣde, -a
Gen.	wina, wini(ge)a	spera	dǣda
Dat.	winum	sperum	dǣdum

Note 1.—Except in very early texts, most masculine i-stems passed into the a-declension. The ending -e in the nom. and acc. pl. is generally kept only in names of peoples, such as **Dene**, *Danes*, and in the five common words **ielde**, *men;* **ielfe**, *elves;* **lēode**, *people;* **stede**, *places;* and **wine**, *friends*.

Note 2.—It will be seen that the neuter i-stems are declined like the neuter a-stems with -e in the nom. and acc. sing. (§ 108, note 4) except that the neuter i-stems have -u in the nom. and acc. pl. whatever the length of the stem-syllable.

Note 3.—It will be seen that the chief difference between the feminine i-stems and the ō-stems is that the former have no inflectional ending in the acc. sing.

u- DECLENSION

111. The **u**-declension comprises masculine and feminine nouns. Most of the nouns that originally belonged to this declension passed into the a- or ō- declensions in primitive Old English, and some nouns are declined both as u-stems, and as a-stems.

Sing.	Masculine		Feminine	
Nom. Acc.	sunu, *son*	feld, *field*	duru, *door*	hand, *hand*
Gen.	suna	felda	dura	handa
Dat.	suna	felda	dura	handa

Pl.				
Nom. Acc.	suna	felda	dura	handa
Gen.	suna	felda	dura	handa
Dat.	sunum	feldum	durum	handum

Masculine nouns, with short stems, declined like **sunu** are: **bregu**, *prince;* **heoru**, *sword;* **lagu**, *sea;* **magu**, *son;* **me(o)du**, *mead;* **si(o)du**, *custom;* **spitu**, *spit;* and **wudu**, *wood.* The feminine noun **nosu**, *nose*, is declined like **duru**.

Masculine nouns, with long stems, declined like **feld** are: **ford**, *ford;* **weald**, *wood.* The feminine nouns **flōr**, *floor*, and **cweorn**, *mill*, are declined like **hand**.

n- DECLENSION

112. This declension includes a large number of masculine and feminine nouns and three neuter nouns.

Sing.	Masculine	Feminine	Neuter
Nom.	guma, *man*	tunge, *tongue*	ēage, *eye*
Acc.	guman	tungan	ēage
Gen.	guman	tungan	ēagan
Dat.	guman	tungan	ēagan

Pl.			
Nom. Acc.	guman	tungan	ēagan
Gen.	gumena	tungena	ēagena
Dat.	gumum	tungum	ēagum

Note 1.—The other two neuter nouns of this declension are **ēare**, *ear*, and **wange**, *cheek* (also declined like the **a**-declension).

Note 2.—The vowel of the inflectional ending is absorbed in a preceding long vowel or diphthong (§ 63). For example, **frēa**, m. *lord*, and **bēo**, f. *bee*, have acc. gen. dat. sing. and nom. acc. pl. **frēan, bēon**, gen. pl. **frēana, bēona**, dat. pl. **frēa(u)m, bēom**.

Note 3.—The noun **oxa**, *ox*, has a nom. acc. pl. **exen** beside **oxan**, gen. pl. **oxna**, and dat. pl. **oxnum**. The noun **nefa**, *nephew*, has dat. pl. **nefenum**.

Note 4.—The ending **-an** is occasionally replaced by **-on**.

MONOSYLLABIC CONSONANT DECLENSION

113. The chief characteristic of nouns of this declension is that some of the oblique cases show front mutation of the stem-vowel. The inflectional ending causing the change has generally disappeared after long stems. There were not many nouns belonging to this declension in Old English, but some of them have remained as a separate declension to the present day.

Sing.	Masculine		Feminine	
Nom. Acc.	fōt, *foot*	mann, *man*	bōc, *book*	hnutu, *nut*
Gen.	fōtes	mannes	bēc	hnute
Dat.	fēt	menn	bēc	hnyte

Pl.				
Nom. Acc.	fēt	menn	bēc	hnyte
Gen.	fōta	manna	bōca	hnuta
Dat.	fōtum	mannum	bōcum	hnutum

Note 1.—The only neuter noun of this class is **scrūd**, *garment*, which has dat. sing. **scrȳd** beside **scrūde;** in other respects this noun is declined like **word** (§ 108). The only other masculine nouns are **wīfmann**, *woman* (declined like **mann**) and **tōþ**, *tooth* (declined like **fōt**). The only other feminine nouns with short stems declined like **hnutu** are **hnitu**, *nit*, and **studu**, *pillar*. Like **bōc** are declined **āc**, *oak;* **brōc**, *breeches;* **burh**, *city* (gen. dat. sing. and nom. acc. pl. **byr(i)g;** see §§ 75, 85) ; **cū**, *cow;* **furh**, *furrow;* **gāt**, *goat;* **gōs**, *goose;* **grūt**, *coarse meal;* **lūs**, *louse;* **meol(u)c**, *milk;* **mūs**, *mouse;* **neaht**, **niht**, *night;* **sulh**, *plough;* **turf**, *turf;* **þrūh**, *trough;* **wlōh**, *fringe*. For the vowels of the mutated oblique cases see § 40.

Note 2.—Analogy is frequent in this declension. Nearly all the feminine nouns have, in addition to forms with mutation, forms without mutation but with the ending -e on the analogy of the ō-declension. In late Old English the dat. sing. was often like the nom. sing. The noun **cū** has gen. sing. **cȳ, cūe, cūs;** nom. acc. pl. **cȳ(e);** gen. pl. **cū(n)a, cȳna.** In **niht** the mutated form with i is usually levelled through the whole declension; the form **neaht** without mutation is rare. An adverbial genitive singular **nihtes**, *by night*, is formed on the analogy of **dæges**, *by day*.

Note 3.—Final **h** of the stem is lost before a vowel in an inflectional ending (§ 98), as in **fura** gen. pl. of **furh.**

STEMS IN -þ

114. Only four nouns belong to this declension in Old English : **hæleþ**, m, *man* ; **mōnaþ**, m. *month* ; **mæg(e)þ**, f. *maiden* ; and **ealu**, n. *ale*.

Sing.

Nom. Acc.	**hæleþ**	**mōnaþ**	**mæg(e)þ**	**ealu**
Gen.	**hæleþes**	**mōn(e)þes**	**mæg(e)þ(e)**	**ealoþ**
Dat.	**hæleþe**	**mōn(e)þe**	**mæg(e)þ(e)**	**ealoþ**

Pl.

Nom. Acc.	**hæleþ,**	**mōnaþ,**	**mæg(e)þ**
	hæleþas	**mōn(e)þas**	
Gen.	**hæleþa**	**mōn(e)þa**	**mæg(e)þa**	**ealeþa**
Dat.	**hæleþum**	**mōn(e)þum**	**mæg(e)þum**

Note 1.—The variant forms of this declension are due to the analogy of other declensions. The gen. sing. of **hæleþ** and **mōnaþ** and the plural forms **hæleþas** and **mōn(e)þas** are due to the analogy of the **a**-declension ; the gen. sing. forms with final -e are due to the analogy of the ō-declension, and the dat. sing. forms with final -e are due to the analogy of both the **a**- and the ō-declensions.

Note 2.—The original type of the nom. and acc. sing. is preserved in **ealu**. An earlier form of the nom. sing. of **hæleþ** is **hæle**, which has gone over to the i-declension (§ 110). In **hæleþ, mōnaþ** and **mæg(e)þ** the þ of the inflected forms has been levelled out into the nom. and acc. sing.

Note 3.—On the syncope of the medial vowel see § 72. The syncope in the inflected forms of **mæg(e)þ** is irregular and has sometimes spread by analogy to the nom. and acc. sing.

STEMS IN -r

115. Five nouns denoting relationship belong to this declension : **fæder**, m. *father;* **brōþor**, m. *brother;* **mōdor**, f. *mother;* **dohtor**, f. *daughter;* and **sweostor**, f. *sister.*

Sing.

Nom. Acc.	fæder	brōþor	mōdor
Gen.	fæder, fæderes	brōþor	mōdor
Dat.	fæder	brēþer	mēder

Pl.

Nom. Acc.	fæderas	brōþor, brōþru	mōdra, mōdru
Gen.	fædera	brōþra	mōdra
Dat.	fæderum	brōþrum	mōdrum

Sing.

Nom. Acc.	dohtor	sweostor
Gen.	dohtor, dehter	sweostor
Dat.	dehter	sweostor

Pl.

Nom. Acc.	dohtor, dohtru	sweostor
Gen.	dohtra	sweostra
Dat.	dohtrum	sweostrum

Note 1.—The gen. sing. **fæderes**, nom. acc. pl. **fæderas** and nom. acc. pl. **brōþru, mōdru** and **dohtru** are due to the analogy of the masculine and neuter nouns of the a-declension.

Note 2.—On the variation between e and o in the lightly stressed syllables see § 73, and on the loss of the lightly stressed vowel see § 72.

Note 3.—It will be seen that no nouns of this declension show front mutation in the plural.

STEMS IN -nd

116. The nouns of this declension, which are nearly all masculine, had their origin in the present participles of verbs.

They fall into two groups : those which, like **frēond**, *friend*, were declined like nouns, and those which, like **wīgend**, *warrior*, had some adjectival endings resulting from their participial origin.

Sing.

Nom. Acc.	**frēond**	**wīgend**
Gen.	**frēondes**	**wīgendes**
Dat.	**friend, frēonde**	**wīgende**

Pl.

Nom. Acc.	**friend, frēond, frēondas**	**wīgend, -e, -as**
Gen.	**frēonda**	**wīgendra**
Dat.	**frēondum**	**wīgendum**

Like **frēond** are declined **fēond**, *enemy;* **tēond**, *accuser;* and **gōddōnd**, *benefactor* (dat. sing. and nom. acc. pl. **gōddēnd**). All other nouns of this declension are declined like **wīgend**, as **wealdend**, *ruler;* **hēēlend**, *Saviour.*

Note.—The gen. sing. in **-es**, the dat. sing. in **-e** and the nom. acc. pl. in **-as** are on the analogy of the masc. **a**-stems. The nom. pl. in **-e** and gen. pl. in **-ra** are adjectival.

IE. **es-, os-** DECLENSION

117. Only six nouns, all of them neuter, remain in this declension, which corresponds to the Greek neuters in **-os** and the Latin neuters in **-us.**

Sing.

Nom. Acc.	**lamb,** *lamb*
Gen.	**lambes**
Dat.	**lambe**

Pl.

Nom. Acc.	**lambru**
Gen.	**lambra**
Dat.	**lambrum**

The other nouns belonging to this declension are : **ǣg**, *egg;* **cealf**, *calf;* **cild**, *child;* **speld**, *splinter;* and **brēadru**, *crumbs.* The last word occurs only in the plural.

Note. 1.—The reason why this is called the **es-, os-** declension is that nouns of this declension in Indo-European had the suffix **-os**, varying with **-es** and **-s.** In Germanic the **s** became **z** by Verner's

Law (§ 77) and this **z** became **r** in West Germanic (§ 79).   The chief characteristic of nouns of this declension in Old English is the **r** in the plural (which has survived in Modern English in the double plural *children*).

Note 2.—In late Old English the plural of **lamb** was **lamb, lamba, lambum** on the analogy of the **a-**stems.   The same analogy gave plural **cild** beside **cildru.**

Note 3.—Many nouns which originally belonged here have passed into other declensions in Old English.   Some of them have retained traces of their origin in the suffix **-er** or **-or** levelled through the paradigm, as **dōgor,** *day;* **hrīþer,** *cattle;* **sigor,** *victory.*

CHAPTER V

ADJECTIVES

STRONG DECLENSION

118. In the strong declension, masculine and neuter adjectives correspond to the **a**-declension of nouns while feminines correspond to the **ō**-declension, but the inflectional endings of certain cases are derived from pronouns. Only a few traces of the **i**- and **u**- declensions of adjectives remain in Old English.

The declension of monosyllabic adjectives may be illustrated by **blind,** *blind;* **glæd,** *glad;* and **hēah,** *high.*

(a) MONOSYLLABIC ADJECTIVES

Sing.	Masculine	Neuter	Feminine
Nom.	blind	blind	blind
Acc.	blindne	blind	blinde
Gen.	blindes	blindes	blindre
Dat.	blindum	blindum	blindre
Instr.	blinde	blinde	

Pl.			
Nom. Acc.	blinde	blind(e)	blinda, -e
Gen.	blindra	blindra	blindra
Dat.	blindum	blindum	blindum

Sing.			
Nom.	glæd	glæd	gladu, -o
Acc.	glædne	glæd	glade
Gen.	glades	glades	glædre
Dat.	gladum	gladum	glædre
Instr.	glade	glade	

Pl.			
Nom. Acc.	glade	gladu, -o, -e	glada, -e
Gen.	glædra	glædra	glædra
Dat.	gladum	gladum	gladum

Sing.	Masculine	Neuter	Feminine
Nom.	hēah	hēah	hēa
Acc.	hēa(n)ne	hēah	hēa
Gen.	hēas	hēas	hēa(r)re
Dat.	hēa(u)m	hēa(u)m	hēa(r)re
Instr.	hēa	hēa	

Pl.			
Nom. Acc.	hēa	hēa	hēa
Gen.	hēa(r)ra	hēa(r)ra	hēa(r)ra
Dat.	hēa(u)m	hēa(u)m	hēa(u)m

Like **blind** are declined long monosyllables, except those ending in **-h**, such as **gōd**, *good;* **lēof**, *dear;* and compound adjectives in **-cund, -fæst, -feald, -full, -lēas, -weard,** such as **ārfæst,** *virtuous;* **andweard,** *present.*

Like **glæd** are declined short monosyllables, such as **hwæt,** *bold.*

Like **hēah** are declined adjectives ending in **h,** such as **fāh,** *hostile;* **þweorh,** *perverse.*

Note 1.—On the variation between **a** and **æ** in **glæd** see §§ 27, 29. On the loss of **h** between vowels in the inflected cases of **hēah** see § 98, and on the assimilation in **hēanne, hēarre,** and **hēarra** see § 90.

Note 2.—It will be seen that the only differences between the inflectional endings of **blind** and those of **glæd** are in the nom. sing. feminine and the nom. and acc. pl. neuter. For the loss of unaccented **-u** or **-o** after long stems see § 69. The forms with final **-e** in the nom. and acc. pl. of the feminine and neuter are found chiefly in later texts and are due to the influence of the masculine. In late Old English, forms of the dat. sing. and pl. in **-un, -on,** and **-an** are found.

Note 3.—Double consonants are simplified before a consonant of the inflectional ending. Examples are **ealne,** acc. sing. masculine, and **ealra,** gen. pl. of **eall,** *all* (§ 101).

Note 4.—Adjectives ending in g often show unvoicing of the g to **h** when it occurs finally (§ 85) though the g is kept in the oblique cases, as in **genōge,** nom. pl. masculine of **genōh,** *enough.* On the analogy of such pairs, late Old English has **hēages,** gen. sing. masculine and neuter, and **hēagum,** dat. pl. of **hēah.**

Note 5.—The adjectives **cwic,** *alive,* and **wlæc,** *tepid,* are declined like **glæd,** but they also have the forms nom. sing. (all genders) **cwicu, c(w)ucu;** **wlacu;** acc. sing. masculine **cucone** (§ 86), survivals of their origin as u-stems. All the other adjectives of the u-declension have passed into other declensions in Old English.

(b) DISSYLLABIC ADJECTIVES

119. The declension of dissyllabic adjectives varies according to the length of the first syllable :

Sing.	Masculine	Neuter	Feminine
Nom.	manig, *many*	manig	manig
Acc.	manigne	manig	manige
Gen.	maniges	maniges	manigre
Dat.	manigum	manigum	manigre
Instr.	manige	manige	

Pl.			
Nom. Acc.	manige	manig	maniga, -e
Gen.	manigra	manigra	manigra
Dat.	manigum	manigum	manigum

Sing.			
Nom.	hālig, *holy*	hālig	hāligu, -o
Acc.	hāligne	hālig	hālge
Gen.	hālges	hālges	hāligre
Dat.	hālgum	hālgum	hāligre
Instr.	hālge	hālge	

Pl.			
Nom. Acc.	hālge	hāl(i)gu, -o	hālga, -e
Gen.	hāligra	hāligra	hāligra
Dat.	hālgum	hālgum	hālgum

Like **manig** are declined most dissyllabic adjectives with short stems, such as **bysig,** *busy;* **fægen,** *glad;* and past participles with short stems like **coren,** *chosen;* **ofslægen,** *slain.*

Like **hālig** are declined dissyllabic adjectives with long stems, such as **gylden,** *golden;* **geōmor,** *sad;* and past participles with long stems like **wunden,** *twisted;* **holpen,** *helped.*

Note.—On the syncope of medial vowels see § 72, and on the loss of final -u see § 69. Before l, syncope often takes place even after short syllables, as in **micel,** *great,* which usually has gen. sing. **micles,** dat. sing. **miclum,** etc.

ja-/jō- STEMS

120. This group consists of adjectives with long stems which in Germanic had the suffix -ja- in the masculine and neuter and -jō- in the feminine.

Sing.	Masculine	Neuter	Feminine
Nom.	wilde, *wild*	wilde	wildu, -o
Acc.	wildne	wilde	wilde
Gen.	wildes	wildes	wildre
Dat.	wildum	wildum	wildre
Instr.	wilde	wilde	
Pl.			
Nom. Acc.	wilde	wildu, -o	wilda, -e
Gen.	wildra	wildra	wildra
Dat.	wildum	wildum	wildum

Like **wilde** are declined a large number of adjectives, such as **æþele,** *noble;* **fǣge,** *fated;* and all present participles. This declension includes a number of adjectives which originally belonged to the **i-**declension. Those with short stems can be recognized by the single medial consonant. If they had belonged to the **ja/jō** declension at the time of the West Germanic doubling of consonants (§ 81), the single consonant would have been doubled. Examples are **gemyne,** *mindful;* **swice,** *deceitful.*

Note 1.—It will be seen that the only differences between the declension of **wilde** and that of **blind** are in the nom. sing. (all genders), and in the acc. sing. and nom. and acc. pl. neuter.

Note 2.—Adjectives which in Germanic had short stems followed by **ja/jō** underwent the West Germanic doubling influence of **j** (§ 81) and are in Old English declined like **blind,** for example, **midd,** *middle.*

121.   **wa-/wō-** STEMS

Sing.	Masculine	Neuter	Feminine
Nom.	gearu, -o, *ready*	gearu, -o	gearu, -o
Acc.	gearone	gearu, -o	gearwe
Gen.	gearwes	gearwes	gearore
Dat.	gear(w)um	gear(w)um	gearore
Instr.	gearwe	gearwe	
Pl.			
Nom. Acc.	gearwe	gearu, -o	gearwa, -e
Gen.	gearora	gearora	gearora
Dat.	gear(w)um	gear(w)um	gear(w)um

Like **gearu** are declined **geolu,** *yellow;* **nearu,** *narrow;* and a few other adjectives.

Note 1.—On the vocalization of **w** to **o** between consonants see § 86, on the vocalization of **w** to **u** when final see § 87, and on the disappearance of **w** before **u** see § 93. In the dative forms ending in **-wum, w** has been re-introduced on the analogy of forms in which it was not followed by **u**. On forms like nom. pl. masculine **gearowe,** gen. sing. **gearuwes,** see § 76.

Note 2.—Adjectives with stems ending in a long vowel or diphthong re-introduced **w** into the nominative from the inflected forms (§ 87) and were declined like **blind** (§ 118). Examples are **glēaw,** *wise;* **slāw,** *slow.* Levelling in two directions has resulted in the following forms of the pl. adj. **fēa(we),** *few:* nom. and acc. masculine **fēa(we),** neuter **fēa;** feminine **fēawa;** gen. **fēa(we)ra;** dat. **fēam, fēa(w)um.**

WEAK DECLENSION

122. The weak declension of adjectives has the same endings as the **n**-declension of nouns (§ 112) except that the adjectives generally have the ending **-ra** instead of **-ena** in the genitive plural.

Sing.	Masculine	Neuter	Feminine
Nom.	blinda, *blind*	blinde	blinde
Acc.	blindan	blinde	blindan
Gen.	blindan	blindan	blindan
Dat.	blindan	blindan	blindan

Pl.			
Nom. Acc.	blindan	blindan	blindan
Gen.	blindra, -ena	blindra, -ena	blindra, -ena
Dat.	blindum	blindum	blindum

For the conditions under which the weak declension is used see § 227. Classes of adjectives which always follow the weak declension are comparatives, superlatives in **-ma,** and all ordinal numerals except **ōþer,** *second.* Superlatives in **-est(e), -ost(e)** are usually declined weak except in the nom. and acc. sing. neuter, which has **-est, -ost** beside **-este, -oste.**

Note 1.—The **ja**-stems and **wa**-stems are declined in the same way: **wilde,** *wild,* and **gearu,** *ready,* have the weak forms nom. sing. masculine **wilda, gearwa,** neuter and feminine **wilde, gearwe.**

Note 2.—Beside the regular dat. pl. in **-um** there also occur forms in **-an.** These forms occur earlier in the weak declension than in the strong (§ 118, note 2) and are probably taken over from the nom. and acc. pl.

Note 3.—In trisyllabic forms the medial vowel remained after short stems but disappeared after long stems (§ 72), as in **fægena, fægene,** *glad,* beside **hālga, hālge,** *holy.*

DECLENSION OF PARTICIPLES

123. Present and past participles, when declined (§§ 221 232) are declined like adjectives and have both strong and weak forms. Present participles are declined like **wilde** (§ 120), and past participles like **manig or hālig** (§ 119) according to the length of the stem-syllable.

COMPARISON OF ADJECTIVES

124. Old English adjectives form their comparatives by the addition of the suffix **-ra** (which sometimes represents an older **-ira** and sometimes **-ōra**) and their superlatives by the addition of **-est** (earlier **-ist**) or **ost** (earlier **-ōst**). The ja-stems and a few **a**-stems had the suffixes containing **i** in primitive Old English and consequently show front mutation of the stem-vowel ; the comparatives and superlatives of most Old English adjectives had suffixes containing **ō** and consequently do not show front mutation.

Examples are :

	Comparative	Superlative
earm, *poor*	**earmra**	**earmost**
glæd, *glad*	**glædra**	**gladost** (§ 27)
clǣne, *clean*	**clǣnra**	**clǣnest**

The following **a**-stems show front mutation in the comparative and superlative :

brād, *broad*	**brǣdra**	**brǣdest**
eald, *old*	**ieldra**	**ieldest**
feorr, *far*	**fierra**	**fierrest**
geong, iung, *young* (§ 83(*b*))	**gingra** (§ 52)	**gingest**
grēat, *great*	**grietra**	**grietest**
hēah, *high*	**hiehra, hierra**	**hiehst**
lang, *long*	**lengra**	**lengest**
sceort, *short*	**scyrtra**	**scyrtest**
strang, *strong*	**strengra**	**strengest**

nēah, *nigh,* has mutation in the superlative **niehst,** but not in the comparative **nēarra; brād** and **hēah** have also forms without mutation **brādra, brādost; hēarra.**

Note 1.—The medial vowel of the superlative is often syncopated, although it is followed by two consonants (§ 72) as **lengsta, hiehsta.**

Note 2.—Forms such as lēofesta beside lēofosta, *dearest*, are due to dissimilation (§ 73).

Note 3.—In late Old English, the superlative ending -ost often becomes -ast or -ust, and these three endings sometimes replace the ending -est of the ja-stems.

Note 4.—Comparatives and superlatives follow the weak declension, except that strong forms are found beside weak in the nom. and acc. sing. neuter of the superlative.

IRREGULAR COMPARISON

125. The following adjectives form their comparatives and superlatives from a different root from that of the positive :

gōd, *good*	bet(e)ra	bet(e)st
	sēlra	sēlest
lӯtel, *little*	lǣssa	lǣst
micel, *great*	māra	mǣst
yfel, *evil*	wiersa	wierrest, wierst

126. A few comparative and superlative adjectives were formed from adverbs : ǣrra, *former*, ǣrest, *first* (cf. ǣr, *before*) ; fyrra, *further*, fyrest, *first* (cf. fore, *before*) ; furþra, *superior* (cf. forþ, *forth*).

127. Old English preserves three examples of an old superlative suffix -um(a), which was added to adverbs and prepositions and which corresponds to the suffix found in Latin prīmus, *first;* summus, *highest*. The Old English examples are : forma, *first;* hindema, *hindmost;* and meduma, medema, *midway*. More often the suffix -est has been added, giving -mest, which is used chiefly to form superlative adjectives from adverbs. Examples are ·

fore, *before*		fyrmest, formest
inne, *within*	innerra	innemest
læt, *late*	lætra	lætemest beside lætest
mid, *middle*		mid(e)mest
niþan, *below*	niþerra	niþemest
sīþ, *late*	sīþra	sīþemest beside sīþest
ufan, *above*	uferra, yferra	ufemest, yfemest
ūt, *out*	ūterra, ӯterra	ūt(e)mest, ӯt(e)mest
norþ, *northwards*	norþerra, nyrþra	norþmest
sūþ, *southwards*	sūþerra, sӯþerra	sūþmest
ēast, *eastwards*	ēasterra	ēastmest
west, *westwards*	westerra	westmest

NUMERALS

128. The Old English numerals are :

	Cardinal	Ordinal
1	ān	forma, formest(a), fyrmest(a), fyrest(a), ǣrest(a)
2	twēgen, tū, twā	ōþer, æfterra
3	þri(e), þrio, þrēo	þridda
4	fēower	fēo(we)rþa
5	fīf	fīfta
6	siex, syx	siexta, syxta
7	seofon	seofoþa
8	eahta	eahtoþa
9	nigon	nigoþa
10	tīen, tȳn, tēn	tēoþa
11	en(d)le(o)fan	en(d)le(o)fta
12	twelf	twelfta
13	þrēotīene	þrēotēoþa
14	fēowertīene	fēowertēoþa
15	fīftīene	fīftēoþa
16	siextīene	siextēoþa
17	seofontīene	seofontēoþa
18	eahtatīene	eahtatēoþa
19	nigontīene	nigontēoþa
20	twĕntig	twĕntigoþa
21	ān and twĕntig	
30	þrītig, þrittig	þrītigoþa
40	fēowertig	fēowertigoþa
50	fīftig	fīftigoþa
60	si(e)xtig	si(e)xtigoþa
70	hundseofontig	hundseofontigoþa
80	hundeahtatig	hundeahtatigoþa
90	hundnigontig	hundnigontigoþa
100	hundtēontig, hund, hundred	hundtēontigoþa
110	hundendlefontig	hundendleftigoþa
120	hundtwelftig	hundtwelftigoþa
200	tū hund, hundred	
300	þrēo hund, hundred	
1000	þūsend	

129. ān was declined according to the strong or weak declension of adjectives. The strong acc. sing. masculine is generally **ǣnne**, later **ænne** (§ 65(c)) beside **ānne**. Strong plural forms are naturally rare, but they occur occasionally with the sense *each, all, every one*, especially in the phrase **ānra gehwylc**, *each one*. When declined weak **āna** means *alone*.

130. twēgen is declined as follows :

	Masculine	Neuter	Feminine
Nom. Acc.	**twēgen**	**tū, twā**	**twā**
Gen. all genders		**twēgea, twēgra**	
Dat. all genders		**twǣm, twām**	

Like **twēgen** is declined **bēgen**, *both*. When the two words are used together, **bā twā** is used for the masculine as well as the feminine. The neuter is **bū tū** or **būtū**.

131. þrī(e) is declined as follows :

	Masculine	Neuter	Feminine
Nom. Acc.	**þrī(e)**	**þrīo, þrēo**	**þrīo, þrēo**
Gen. all genders		**þrīora, þrēora**	
Dat. all genders		**þrim**	

132. The cardinal numerals 4 to 19 generally remain uninflected when they stand before a noun ; when they follow a noun and when they are used as nouns they are declined like the plurals of nouns of the **i**-declension ; nom. and acc. m. and f. **-e**, n. **-u;** gen. **-a,** dat. **-um.**

133. The ending **-tig** of the numerals from 20 to 120 was originally a noun ; the Old English numerals in **-tig** could be used either as nouns or as adjectives. When they are used as nouns the genitive ends in **-es;** when used as adjectives they are either uninflected or declined like **manig** (§ 119). Since they were originally nouns, numerals in **-tig**, like **hund** and **þūsend**, may be followed by a noun in the partitive genitive. Examples are **fīftiges elna lang,** *fifty ells long;* **twentig scēapa,** *twenty sheep.* **hund,** *hundred,* is generally uninflected, but it occasionally has dative forms in **-e, -um. þūsend,** *thousand,* is sometimes uninflected but is more often declined as a neuter noun.

134. The ordinal numbers **formest(a), fyrmest(a), fyrest(a)** may follow either the strong or the weak declension ; **ōþer**

is always strong ; the other ordinal numbers are all inflected like weak adjectives.

135. Multiplicative adjectives are formed by adding **-feald** to the numerals, and are declined like ordinary adjectives. The first element of **twifeald**, *twofold*, and **þrifeald**, *threefold*, is sometimes inflected, as in dat. **twǣmfealdum**, **þrimfealdum**.

CHAPTER VI

PRONOUNS AND ADVERBS

PERSONAL PRONOUNS

136.

FIRST PERSON

	Singular	Dual	Plural
Nom.	ic, *I*	wit	wē
Acc.	mec, mē	unc, uncit	ūsic, ūs
Gen.	mīn	uncer	ūser, ūre
Dat.	mē	unc	ūs

SECOND PERSON

	Singular	Dual	Plural
Nom.	þū, *thou*	git	gē
Acc.	þec, þē	inc, incit	ēowic, ēow, īow
Gen.	þīn	incer	ēower, īower
Dat.	þē	inc	ēow, īow

THIRD PERSON
Singular

	Masculine	Neuter	Feminine
Nom.	hē, *he*	hit	hīo, hēo
Acc.	hine, hiene	hit	hīe, hī, hȳ
Gen.	his	his	hire, hiere, hyre
Dat.	him	him	hire, hiere, hyre

Plural (all genders)

Nom. Acc.	hīe, hī, hȳ
Gen.	hira, hiera, hiora, heora
Dat.	him

Note 1.—When forms have both long and short vowels, those with long vowels are the strongly stressed, and those with short vowels the lightly stressed forms.

Note 2.—The accusative forms **mec, þec, ūsic, ēowic** occurred only in early texts and in poetry. Later they were replaced by the dative forms **mē, þē, ūs, ēow.**

Note 3.—The gen. pl. forms **hiora, heora** are due to back mutation (§ 45). The **eo** sometimes spread by analogy to the dat. pl. giving **heom**. The acc. sing. masculine **hiene**, gen. and dat. sing. feminine **hiere** and gen. pl. **hiera** are inverted spellings (§ 10).

Note 4.—Forms with **ȳ** for īe are found especially in later texts (§ 51) ; **hig** is sometimes used as a spelling for **hī** (§ 10).

POSSESSIVE PRONOUNS

137. In the main the Old English possessive pronouns are based upon the genitive forms of the personal pronouns. They are declined like strong adjectives : **mīn, þīn** like **blind ; ūser, ēower, uncer, incer** like **hālig;** and **ūre** like **wilde,** except that the nom. sing. feminine is **ūre** and that forms with **-rr-** often undergo simplification to **-r-** (§ 103), since pronouns are often lightly stressed. For the possessive pronoun of the third person the old reflexive **sīn** is sometimes used in poetry, rarely in prose, and is declined like a strong adjective. More often the genitive forms of the personal pronoun, **his, hiere, hiera,** are used, and these are never declined.

Note.—In the declension of **ūser, sr** was usually assimilated to **ss** (§ 90), and then the **ss** was sometimes extended by analogy to other forms in place of **s.** Examples are gen. pl. **ūssa** beside **ūsra** and analogical **ūssera,** gen. sing. **ūsses.**

DEMONSTRATIVE PRONOUNS

138. The simple demonstrative pronoun is used also as the definite article :

	Masculine	Neuter	Feminine
		Singular	
Nom.	sē	þæt	sio, sēo
Acc.	þone	þæt	þā
Gen.	þæs	þæs	þǣre
Dat.	þǣm, þām	þǣm, þām	þǣre
Instr.	þȳ, þon	þȳ, þon	

	Plural (all genders)
Nom. Acc.	þā
Gen.	þāra, þǣra
Dat.	þǣm, þām

Note 1.—**ǣ** belongs to the dat. sing. masculine and neuter and to the dat. pl. and has been borrowed thence into the gen. pl. and gen. and dat. sing. feminine. Similarly **ā** has spread from the nom. acc. and gen. pl. into the dat. pl. and the dat. sing. masculine and neuter. The gen. and dat. sing. feminine **þere** is preserved only in non-West Saxon dialects.

Note 2.—In late texts we often find **þas** for **þæs, þæne** and **þane** for **þone** and **þāre** for **þǣre.**

139. The compound demonstrative pronoun was originally formed from the simple demonstrative by the addition of the particle **-se, -si.**

Singular

	Masculine	Neuter	Feminine
Nom.	þes	þis	þīos, þēos
Acc.	þisne	þis	þās
Gen.	þis(s)es	þis(s)es	þisse
Dat.	þis(s)um	þis(s)um	þisse
Instr.	þȳs, þīs	þȳs, þīs	

Plural (all genders)

Nom. Acc.	þās
Gen.	þissa
Dat.	þis(s)um

140. **ilca,** *same,* occurs only in combination with the definite article and follows the weak declension of adjectives, **self,** *self,* is used either alone or in apposition to another pronoun (§ 230) and is declined both strong and weak. Examples are **hē selfa,** *he himself;* **selfe ofersāwon,** *they themselves looked on.*

INTERROGATIVE PRONOUNS

141. The simple interrogative pronoun is declined in the singular only, and the masculine form is used for both masculine and feminine pronouns.

	Masculine	Neuter
Nom.	hwā, *who*	hwæt, *what*
Acc.	hwone, hwane, hwæne	hwæt
Gen.	hwæs	hwæs
Dat.	hwǣm, hwām	hwǣm, hwām
Instr.		hwȳ, hwī, hwon

142. Other interrogative pronouns are : **hwæþer,** *which of two;* **hwelc, hwilc, hwylc,** *which, what sort of,* and **hūlic,** *of what kind.* They are declined according to the strong declension of adjectives.

INDEFINITE PRONOUNS

143. Indefinite pronouns were freely formed from the interrogative pronouns by the addition of various prefixes and suffixes. The interrogative pronouns **hwā, hwæþer** and **hwilc** are also used alone as indefinite pronouns. Examples are :

(*a*) With the prefix **ā-** : **āhwā**, *any one;* **āhwæþer, ōhwæþer, āwþer, ōwþer,** *one of two;* **nāhwæþer, nōhwæþer, nāwþer, nōwþer,** *neither of two.*

(*b*) With the prefix **ge-** (older **gi-**) : **gehwā**, *each one;* **gehwæþer,** *each of two;* **gehwilc,** *each.*

(*c*) With the double prefix **æg-** (older **ā-gi-**) : **æghwā,** *each one ;* **æghwæþer,** *each of two ;* **æghwilc,** *each one.*

(*d*) With the suffix **-hwugu: hwæthwugu,** *something;* **hwelchwugu,** *some one.*

144. Phrases containing interrogative pronouns are used as indefinite pronouns :

(*a*) **swā hwā swā,** *whoever;* **swā hwæt swā,** *whatever;* **swā hwæþer swā,** *whichever of two;* **swā hwelc swā,** *whichever.*

(*b*) **nāt hwā,** *someone;* **nāt hwæt,** *something;* **nāt hwelc,** *someone.*

(*c*) **lōc hwæþer,** *whichever;* **lōc hwæt,** *whatever.*

145. Other indefinite pronouns are : **ælc,** *each;* **ænig,** *any;* **nænig,** *no one;* **ān,** *someone;* **nān,** *no one;* **āwiht, ōwiht, āwuht, ōwuht, āht, ōht,** *anything;* **nāwiht, nōwiht, nāwuht, nāht, nōht,** *nothing;* **man,** *one;* **sum,** *some one;* **swelc, swilc,** *such;* **þyslic, þuslic, þyllic, þullic,** *such.*

146. Adverbs were formed from adjectives in Old English by the addition of the suffix **-e,** which is identical in origin with the **-e** found in the instrumental case of adjectives. Examples are **georne,** *willingly,* beside **georn,** *willing;* **sweotole,** *clearly,* beside **sweotol,** *clear*; **gearwe,** *completely,* beside **gearu,** *ready.*

When the adjective ends in **-e,** the adverb and adjective are alike in form, as **blīþe,** *joyfully,* beside **blīþe,** *joyful.*

Note.—Some adjectives have double forms derived from the same root, one an **a**-stem without front mutation and the other a **ja**-stem with front mutation. Examples are **smōþ, smēþe,** *smooth;* **sōft, sēfte,** *soft;* **swōt, swēte,** *sweet.* Adverbs formed from such adjectives have final **-e** without front mutation of the stem-vowel, as **smōþe,** *smoothly;* **sōfte,** *softly;* **swōte,** *sweetly.*

147. Adverbs were formed from adjectives in **-līc** by the addition of the suffix **-e,** as **luflīce,** *lovingly;* **frēondlīce,**

in a friendly manner. In such words the **-līce** came to be regarded as an adverbial ending, and it was then used in forming adverbs from adjectives which did not end in **-līc,** as **eornostlīce,** *indeed.*

148. A few adverbs have the ending **-a,** which goes back to an old ablative ending, as **sōna,** *immediately;* **tela,** *well;* **twiwa,** *twice.* The same ending is preserved in the combinations **-inga, -unga,** as in **eallunga,** *altogether;* **fǣringa, fǣrunga,** *suddenly;* **hōlunga,** *without cause.*

149. Many adverbs were formed from the oblique cases of nouns and adjectives :

acc. sing. **eall,** *altogether;* **ealne weg, ealneg,** *always;* **ful,** *completely;*

gen. sing. **dæges,** *by day;* **innanbordes,** *at home;*

dat. sing. **elne,** *vigorously;* **micle,** *greatly;*

gen. pl. **geāra,** *long ago;* **ungeāra,** *recently;*

dat. pl. **hwīlum,** *at times;* **styccemǣlum,** *here and there;* **wundrum,** *wonderfully.*

150. Adverbs were frequently formed by combining prepositions with nouns, adjectives, or adverbs, either as phrases or as compound words, as **mid ealle,** *altogether;* **ofdūne,** *down;* **to āhte,** *at all;* **tōdæg,** *today;* **onweg,** *away.*

151. In adverbs of place the suffix **-or** is often used to indicate motion towards and **-an** to indicate motion from, but **-an** is sometimes found in adverbs expressing rest, and motion towards is sometimes expressed by an adverb without suffix. Examples are :

Rest	Motion towards	Motion from
feorr, *far, afar*	**feorr**	**feorran**
hēr, *here*	**hider**	**hionan**
hwǣr, *where*	**hwider**	**hwonan**
inne, *within*	**in(n)**	**innan**
nēah, *near*	**nēar**	**nēan**
nioþan, *beneath*	**niþer**	**nioþan**
þǣr, *there*	**þider**	**þonan**
uppe, *up, above*	**ūp(p)**	**uppan**
ūte, *outside*	**ūt**	**ūtan**

COMPARISON OF ADVERBS

152. The comparative of adverbs is generally expressed by **-or** and the superlative by **-ost,** as **earme,** *miserably,* **earmor, earmost;** **oft,** *often,* **oftor, oftost.**

153. A few adverbs in Germanic had comparatives in **-iz** and superlatives in **-ist**. In Old English these adverbs show front mutation of the stem-vowel in the comparative and superlative. The comparative suffix **-iz** disappears in Old English while the superlative **-ist** appears in Old English as **-est**. Examples are :

feorr, *far*	**fierr**	**fierrest**
lange, *long*	**leng**	**lengest**
ēaþe, *easily*	**īeþ**	
sōfte, *softly*	**sēft**	

Four adverbs have comparatives and superlatives formed in this way from a stem different from that of the positive :

lȳt, *little*	**lǣs**	**lǣst**
micle, *much*	**mǣ, mā**	**mǣst**
wel, *well*	**bet**	**betst**
	sēl	**sēlest**
yf(e)le, *badly*	**wiers, wyrs**	**wierrest, wyrst**

CHAPTER VII

VERBS

154. Most Old English verbs fall into one of two large classes, the strong and the weak. Strong verbs form their preterites by changing the vowel of the stem; weak verbs do so by the addition of a suffix containing a dental or a post-dental consonant. Beside these large classes there are some verbs, few in number but of frequent occurrence, which have to be regarded as irregular.

155. There are only two simple tenses in Old English, present and preterite. Future time is generally expressed by the present tense, but we find in Old English the beginnings of the use of auxiliary verbs to express compound tenses (§ 232). A trace of the old passive voice is preserved in **hātte**, *is called*, *was called*, pl. **hātton.** Usually in Old English the passive is expressed by means of the auxiliaries **bēon** or **wesan**, *to be*, or **weorþan**, *to become*, used with the past participle (§ 233).

STRONG VERBS

156. The variations of stem-vowel in strong verbs are of two kinds : those which result from sound-changes in Germanic or Old English, and those which existed in Indo-European, to which the name ablaut is given. Ablaut, or gradation, is not confined to strong verbs—it is found, for example, in such pairs as **dæg** beside **dōgor**, *day;* **fōt**, *foot*, beside **feter**, *fetter*—but ablaut variation is illustrated most clearly in the strong verbs. Four forms, called the principal parts, are enough to enable one to give the complete conjugation of any strong verb. They are : (1) the infinitive, (2) the 1 sing. pret. ind., which is identical in form with the 3 sing. pret. ind., (3) the plural of the pret. ind., and (4) the past participle. The representative verbs **beran**, *to carry;* **helpan**, *to help;* **biddan**, *to pray;* **slēan**, *to strike;* and **bindan**, *to bind*, will serve to show how a complete conjugation can be built up on the basis of the four principal parts.

59

PRESENT
Indicative

Sing.					
1.	bere	helpe	bidde	slēa	binde
2.	bir(e)st	hilpst	bitst	sliehst	bintst
3.	bir(e)þ	hilpþ	bit(t)	sliehþ	bint

Pl.					
	beraþ	helpaþ	biddaþ	slēaþ	bindaþ

Subjunctive

Sing.					
	bere	helpe	bidde	slēa	binde

Pl.					
	beren	helpen	bidden	slēan	binden

Imperative

Sing.					
2.	ber	help	bide	sleah	bind

Pl.					
2.	beraþ	helpaþ	biddaþ	slēaþ	bindaþ

Infinitive

	beran	helpan	biddan	slēan	bindan

Participle

	berende	helpende	biddende	slēande	bindende

PRETERITE
Indicative

Sing.					
1.	bær	healp	bæd	slōh, slōg	band
2.	bǣre	hulpe	bǣde	slōge	bunde
3.	bær	healp	bæd	slōh, slōg	band

Pl.					
	bǣron	hulpon	bǣdon	slōgon	bundon

Subjunctive

Sing.					
	bǣre	hulpe	bǣde	slōge	bunde

Pl.					
	bǣren	hulpen	bǣden	slōgen	bunden

Participle

	geboren	geholpen	gebeden	geslǣgen	gebunden

THE ENDINGS OF STRONG VERBS

157. *Present Indicative.* The original ending of the first person sing. was -ō (cf. Latin **amō,** *I love*), which became **-u** in primitive Old English. This ending was preserved in Anglian, even after long stems, where it is due to the analogy of verbs with short stems (§ 69), as in **bindu,** *I bind* on the analogy of forms like **beru,** *I carry.* In West Saxon and Kentish the **-u** was replaced by the ending **-e** from the pres. subj. The ending of the second person sing. in primitive Old English was **-is** and that of the third person sing. **-iþ.** The final **-t** of the 2 sing. arose partly from the preterite-present verbs (§ 199) and partly from mis-division of forms in which the personal pronoun followed the verb and was attached to it, such as **bindesþu,** later **bindestu,** *dost thou bind.* The **i** of the ending of the 2, 3 sing. pres. ind. caused front mutation (or the earlier change of **e** to **i** described in § 19) of the stem-vowel and then normally disappeared after long stems but was weakened to **e** after short stems (§§ 70, 72). Forms like **birst, birþ,** from **beran,** *to carry,* are due to the analogy of verbs with long stems, and are especially common in West Saxon, whereas Anglian tends to generalize forms without syncope and with an unmutated stem-vowel, such as **hāteþ,** *he calls.*

On the unvoicing of **d** to **t** in 2 sing. pres. ind. **bitst, bintst,** 3 sing. **bit(t), bint** and on the assimilation of **tþ** to **tt** in **bitt** and * **bintt** see § 90 ; on the subsequent simplification of **tt** see § 101.

158. *Present Subjunctive.* In the plural beside **-en** there occur in later texts the endings **-an, -on.** The final **-n** of the subjunctive plural disappeared in West Saxon and Kentish when a personal pronoun of the first or second person immediately followed the verb, as **bere wē, bere gē.** Then forms with **-e** spread by analogy to the indicative when the verb was followed by a pronoun, as **bere gē** beside **gē beraþ.**

159. *Imperative.* In Old English the imperative singular is normally the bare stem of the word, and in most verbs may be obtained by removing the **-an** ending of the infinitive. Strong verbs whose infinitives ended in **-jan** in Germanic (§ 160) had **-i** in the imperative singular. This **i** did not cause doubling of a preceding consonant in West Germanic (§ 81, Note 2) and appears in Old English as **-e,** as in **bide,** 2 sing. imper. of **biddan,** *to pray;* **site,** 2 sing. imper. of **sittan,** *to sit.*

160. *Infinitive.* The infinitive was originally a neuter noun. A trace of this origin is seen in a dative singular, sometimes called a gerund, formed on the model of **ja**-stem nouns and used after the preposition **tō**, as **tō berenne,** from **beran,** *to carry* (§ 238). The ending **-enne** later became **-anne** through the influence of the infinitive ending **-an.** In later Old English the **nn** was often simplified and we find **-ene, -ane** (§ 103).

A few strong verbs had the ending **-jan** in the infinitive in Germanic. These can be recognized by the front mutation of the stem-vowel and, when the stem was originally short, by the doubling of the medial consonant (§ 81). The **j** disappeared since the stem, if originally short, became long as a result of the doubling of the consonant (§ 95). Examples are **biddan,** *to pray;* **sittan,** *to sit;* **wēpan,** *to weep.*

161. *Preterite Subjunctive.* The final **-n** of the plural disappeared in West Saxon and Kentish when a personal pronoun of the first or second person immediately followed the verb, as **bēre wē.** Then forms with **-e** came to be used also for the indicative when the pronoun followed (cf. § 158).

162. *Past Participle.* The most common ending of the pp. of strong verbs is **-en,** which has two origins. The usual origin is Gmc. **-an-.** The vowel of the Old English ending **-en** was levelled from the oblique cases where the **n** was followed by a vowel and therefore belonged to the next syllable ; in the infinitive the **a** remained (§ 71). A less common origin of OE. **-en** in pps. is Gmc. **-in-** ; pps. with front mutation, like **gecymen** (§ 179), **geslegen** (§ 186), are of this origin. The past participle of both strong and weak verbs is found both with and without the prefix **ge-,** as **bunden** beside **gebunden,** *bound;* the prefix **ge-** is avoided if the verb already has another prefix, as **forboden,** *forbidden.* Some verbs have the prefix **ge-** throughout their conjugation. Its original function was to express completeness, and in Old English it is often used to describe the result of the action described by the simple verb, as in **gesittan,** *to take possession of,* beside **sittan,** *to sit;* **gefrignan,** *to learn,* beside **frignan,** *to ask.*

THE CLASSIFICATION OF STRONG VERBS

163. Old English strong verbs are divided into seven classes. Old English sound-changes have obscured the original ablaut relationship in many verbs, but it is usually an easy matter to assign a strong verb to its correct class. Strong verbs of class I had, in primitive Old English, the stem-vowel ī in the infinitive ; those of class II had ēo or ū; those of classes III, IV and V usually had e; those of class VI had a; those of class VII had a variety of vowels and demand special attention (§§ 188-190). It is possible to assign verbs of classes III, IV and V to their correct classes by noticing the medial consonant : in class III the stem ends with a group of two consonants ; in class IV it ends with a single liquid or nasal ; in class V it ends with a single consonant other than a liquid or nasal.

CLASS I

164. The regular type is represented by :

    bīdan, *to wait for*   **bād**   **bidon**   **gebiden**

Many verbs are conjugated like **bīdan**. Among them are **bītan,** *to bite;* **gewītan,** *to depart;* **wrītan,** *to write.*

165. The principal parts of **līþan,** *to go,* are **līþan, lāþ, lidon, geliden,** and **scrīþan,** *to go,* and **snīþan,** *to cut,* are conjugated in the same way. In the pret. pl. and pp. of strong verbs the accent in Germanic was on the ending. Hence the **d** in **lidon** and **geliden** is to be explained by Verner's Law (§ 77) and the subsequent change of the voiced fricative [ð] to the plosive **d** (§ 80). In other verbs of class I the **þ** or **s** of the present was extended by analogy to all forms of the verb, as in **ārīsan,** *to arise;* **wrīþan,** *to twist.*

166. tēon, *to accuse*   **tāh**   **tigon**   **getigen**

Like **tēon** go **lēon,** *to lend;* **sēon,** *to sift;* **þēon,** *to prosper;* **wrēon,** *to cover.* These verbs had stems ending with the fricative **h** in Germanic. The **ēo** in the infinitive is from earlier **īo,** which arose from **ī** by fracture (§ 32(*d*)) before **h,** which later disappeared between vowels (§ 98). The **g** of the preterite plural and past participle arose from **h** by Verner's Law (§ 77).

Note.—Verbs of this type often formed their pret. pl. and pp. on the analogy of verbs of class II, as **tēon, tēah, tugon, getogen.**

CLASS II

167. The regular type is represented by :

    bēodan, *to command*   **bēad**   **budon**   **geboden**

Like **bēodan** go many verbs including **gēotan,** *to pour;* **scēotan,** *to shoot.*

168. Verbs with **s** in the infinitive have **r** in the pret. pl. and pp. (§§ 77, 79) and those with **þ** have **d** (§§ 77, 80).

cēosan, *to choose*	cēas	curon	gecoren

Similarly **drēosan**, *to fall;* **forlēosan**, *to lose;* **frēosan**, *to freeze;* **hrēosan**, *to fall;* **sēoþan**, *to boil* (**sēaþ, sudon, gesoden**).

169. | **flēon**, *to flee* | **flēah** | **flugon** | **geflogen** |

Similarly, **tēon**, *to draw*. These verbs differ from the contracted verbs of class I in that the diphthong **ēo** in class I arose by fracture in primitive Old English whereas in class II it was derived from a Germanic diphthong.

170. A few verbs of class II have **ū** in the present :

būgan, *to bow*	bēag	bugon	gebogen

Similarly **brūcan**, *to enjoy;* **dūfan**, *to dive;* **scūfan**, *to push*.

CLASS III

171. The regular type is represented by :

bregdan, *to move quickly*	brægd	brugdon	gebrogden
berstan, *to burst*	bærst	burston	geborsten

stregdan, *to strew*, is conjugated like **bregdan**. These two verbs also have forms with loss of **g** and lengthening of the preceding vowel, as **brēdan, brǣd, brūdon, gebrōden** (§ 99). **þerscan**, *to thresh*, is conjugated like **berstan**. There is no fracture in these two verbs because at the time when fracture took place the **r** preceded the stem-vowel and there has since been metathesis (§ 91).

172. Verbs whose stems ended in a nasal + consonant have **i** in the infin. (§ 18), **a** or **o** in the pret. sing. (§ 24), and **u** in the pret. pl. and pp. (§ 20).

bindan, *to bind*	band, bond	bundon	gebunden

Similarly many verbs including **climban**, *to climb;* **drincan**, *to drink;* **findan**, *to find* (pret. sing. also **funde** from the subjunctive).

*Note 1.—***irnan**, *to run*, **arn** (also **orn, earn**), **urnon, geurnen**, and **birnan**, *to burn*, **barn** (also **born, bearn**), **burnon, geburnen** show metathesis (§ 91) ; cf. Gothic **rinnan, brinnan**.

*Note 2.—***frignan**, *to ask*, has the principal parts **frignan, frægn, frugnon, gefrugnen**. It also has forms with loss of **g** and lengthening of the stem-vowel: **frinan, frān, frūnon, gefrūnen** (§ 99); **frān** is on the analogy of verbs of class I.

173. Verbs whose stems end in l + a consonant have **ea** by fracture in the 1 and 3 sing. pret. ind. (§ 32(*a*)).

| helpan, *to help* | healp | hulpon | geholpen |

Similarly **belgan,** *to be angry;* **delfan,** *to dig;* **meltan,** *to melt;* **swelgan,** *to swallow;* **swellan,** *to swell;* **sweltan,** *to die.*

*Note.—***feolan,** *to enter,* from **feolhan (§ 98) has principal parts **fealh, fulgon, gefolgen,** with **h** varying with **g** by Verner's Law (§ 77). It also has pret. pl. **fulon,** from **fulhon (with **h** replacing **g** on the analogy of the infin. or pret. sing.), and pret. pl. **fǣlon,** pp. **gefolen** on the analogy of verbs of class IV.

174. Verbs with initial **g** whose stems end in l + a consonant have **ie** in the infin. (§ 36) and **ea** in the 1 and 3 sing. pret. ind. (§ 32(*a*)).

| gieldan, *to pay* | geald | guldon | gegolden |

Similarly **giellan,** *to yell;* **gielpan,** *to boast.*

*Note.—*Since fracture took place earlier than front diphthongization (§ 37), the **ea** in pret. **geald** is probably due to the influence of fracture (§ 32(*a*)), although front diphthongization (§ 36) would have produced the same result.

175. Verbs whose stems end in **r** + consonant or **h** + consonant have **eo** in the infinitive and **ea** in the pret. sing.

beorgan, *to protect*	bearg	burgon	geborgen
feohtan, *to fight*	feaht	fuhton	gefohten
weorþan, *to become*	wearþ	wurdon	geworden

Similarly **ceorfan,** *to carve;* **steorfan,** *to die;* **weorpan,** *to throw.* On the alternation between **þ** and **đ** in the conjugation of **weorþan** see §§ 77, 80.

176. Two verbs of this class have **u** in the infinitive. They are :

murnan, *to mourn*	mearn	murnon	gemurnen
spurnan, spornan			
to spurn	spearn	spurnon	gespurnen

CLASS IV

177. The regular type is represented by :

| beran, *to bear* | bær | bǣron | geboren |

Similarly **stelan,** *to steal;* **helan,** *to conceal;* and a few others.

178. In **scieran**, *to cut*, the stem-vowel underwent front diphthongization (§ 36) :

scieran	scear	scēaron	gescoren

179. Two verbs have stems ending in a single nasal :

niman, *to take*	nōm	nōmon	genumen
cuman, *to come*	c(w)ōm	c(w)ōmon	gecumen

Note 1.—The **i** in **niman** is from earlier **e** by the influence of the following nasal (§ 25) ; the **u** of **cuman** represents a different grade of vowel in Indo-European (§ 156). On the **ō** in the pret. pl. see § 23, and on the **u** in the pp. see § 26. On the disappearance of **w** in **cōmon**, see § 93. The **ō** in the pret. sing. **nōm** (beside **nam**) and **c(w)ōm** is due to the analogy of the pl., perhaps re-inforced by verbs of strong class VI.

Note 2.—In the present subjunctive of **cuman** the forms **cyme, cymen** occur beside **cume, cumen**. A past participle **gecymen** is found with front mutation (§ 162).

CLASS V

180. The regular type is represented by :

metan, *to measure*	mæt	mǣton	gemeten

Similarly **brecan**, *to break;* **drepan**, *to strike;* **wrecan**, *to avenge;* and other verbs, except that **brecan** and **drepan** sometimes have **o** in the pp. on the analogy of class IV. **etan**, *to eat*, and **fretan**, *to devour*, are conjugated like **metan** except that they have **ǣ** in the pret. sing. : **ǣt, frǣt.**

181. **giefan**, *to give*   **geaf**   **gēafon**   **gegiefen**
Similarly **forgietan**, *to forget;* **ongietan**, *to understand*. In these verbs the diphthongs are due to the influence of the preceding palatal consonant (§ 36).

182. Some verbs show variations resulting from Verner's Law and subsequent changes (see §§ 77, 79, 80).

cweþan, *to say*	cwæþ	cwǣdon	gecweden
wesan, *to be*	wæs	wǣron	

In **genesan**, *to be saved*, and **lesan**, *to gather*, the **s** of the present and pret. sing. has been extended to all forms.

183. A few verbs show Verner's Law variation with loss of **h** between vowels (see §§ 77, 98).

sēon, *to see*	seah	sāwon, sǣgon	gesewen, gesegen, gesawen
gefēon, *to rejoice*	gefeah	gefǣgon	gefegen

plēon, *to risk*, goes like **gefēon.**

Note.—The medial consonant in the principal parts of **sēon** was originally a labio-velar. When it was followed in Germanic by a back rounded vowel (as in the pret. ind. pl.), the labio-velar lost its labial element and became **g**; in other positions (as in the pret. subj. and pp.) it lost its velar element and became **w**. The pret. pl. **sāwon** and pp. **gesegen** are analogical.

184. A few verbs had the ending **-jan** in the infinitive in Germanic (§ 160). The **j** caused doubling of the preceding consonant and front mutation of the stem-vowel, and later disappeared (§§ 81, 39).

biddan, *to pray*	**bæd**	**bǣdon**	**gebeden**
sittan, *to sit*	**sæt**	**sǣton**	**geseten**
licgan, *to lie*	**læg**	**lǣgon**	**gelegen**

fricgan, *to ask,* goes like **licgan** except that it has pp. **gefregen, gefrigen. þicgan,** *to receive,* in poetry has the strong forms **þeah** (on the analogy of **gefeah**), **þǣgon, geþegen;** in prose it is a weak verb with preterite **þig(e)de.**

CLASS VI

185. The regular type is represented by :

faran, *to go*   **fōr** **fōron**   **gefaren, gefæren**

Similarly **galan,** *to sing;* **wadan,** *to go;* and others. The following irregularities may be noted :

(a) Verbs with initial **sc-** often have an intrusive **e** (§ 9), as **sc(e)acan,** *to shake;* **sc(e)ōc, sc(e)ōcon, gesc(e)acen,** and similarly **sc(e)afan,** *to shave.*

(b) **standan,** *to stand,* **stōd, stōdon, gestanden** has a nasal infix, introduced into the pp. from the present, of the kind found in Latin **vinco** beside **vīci.**

(c) **spanan,** *to entice,* **spōn, spōnon, gespanen** has also a pret. **spēon, spēonon** on the analogy of the verb **spannan,** *to clasp,* in class VII.

186. A few verbs show Verner's Law variation with loss of **h** between vowels in the infinitive (§§ 77, 98) :

slēan, *to strike*   **slōh, slōg** **slōgon**   **geslægen, geslagen**

Similarly **flēan,** *to flay;* **lēan,** *to blame;* **þwēan,** *to wash.* Beside the pps. with **æ** and **a** there occur a few pps. with front mutation, as **geslegen, geþwegen** (§ 162).

187. A few verbs had the ending -jan in the infinitive in Germanic (§ 160) :

hebban, *to raise*	hōf	hōfon	gehæfen, gehafen
sceppan, *to injure*	scōd	scōdon	
steppan, *to step*	stōp	stōpon	gestæpen, gestapen
hliehhan, *to laugh*	hlōh, hlōg	hlōgon	
scieppan, *to create*	scōp	scōpon	gesceapen
swerian, *to swear*	swōr	swōron	gesworen

On the variation between **bb** and **f** in **hebban** see § 81, Note 1. On the absence of doubling in **swerian** see § 81. **sceppan** and **hliehhan** show Verner's Law variations (§§ 77, 80) ; the **d** in **scōd** and the **g** in **hlōg** are on the analogy of the pl. The infinitive **sceppan** is a non-West Saxon form ; in West Saxon the **e** would normally become **ie** (§ 36). The pp. **gesworen** has **o** on the analogy of verbs of class IV. **hebban,** **sceppan,** and **swerian** have weak preterites **hefde, scepede, swerede** beside the strong forms.

CLASS VII

188. Some verbs of this class once formed their preterites by reduplication, like Gothic **laílōt,** pret. of **lētan,** *to allow.* In learning this conjugation it is usually necessary to remember only two principal parts, since the vowel of the pret. sing. is identical with that of the pret. pl. and the vowel of the infin. is usually identical with that of the pp. Verbs of this class show a variety of vowels in the infinitive; they are divided into two groups according as the preterite had **ē** or **ēo**.

Traces of the old reduplication are preserved in Anglian and in poetry. Examples are **heht,** pret. of **hātan,** *to call, command;* **leolc,** pret. of **lācan,** *to move, play;* **leort,** pret. of **lētan,** WS. **lǣtan,** *to allow;* **ondreord,** pret. of **ondrēdan,** WS. **ondrǣdan,** *to fear;* and **reord,** pret. of **rēdan,** WS. **rǣdan,** *to advise.* The more usual WS. forms are given in § 189.

189.   DIVISION I : PRETERITES IN ē

(a) **lǣtan,** *to allow*	lēt	lēton	gelǣten
(b) **hātan,** *to command*	hēt	hēton	gehāten
(c) **fōn,** *to seize*	fēng	fēngon	gefangen
(d) **blandan,** *to mingle*	blēnd	blēndon	geblanden

Like **lǣtan** go **ondrǣdan**, *to fear;* **rǣdan**, *to advise;* and **slǣpan**, *to sleep.* These verbs have also weak preterites **ondrǣdde**, **rǣdde**, **slǣpte**, especially in late WS.

Like **hātan** go **lācan**, *to play;* and **sc(e)ādan**, *to divide,* with a preterite **scēad** beside **scēd**; weak forms occur in Anglian.

Note.—Like **fōn** goes **hōn**, *to hang.* For the forms **fōn**, **hōn**, older * **fanhan**, * **hanhan**, see §§ 98, 21. **fēng**, **hēng** are new formations on the analogy of the plural, where the g results from Verner's Law (§ 77).

190. DIVISION II : PRETERITES IN **ēo**

(*a*) **healdan**, *to hold*	**hēold**	**hēoldon**	**gehealden**
(*b*) **spannan**, *to fasten*	**spēon(n)**	**spēonnon**	**gespannen**
(*c*) **bēatan**, *to beat*	**bēot**	**bēoton**	**gebēaten**
(*d*) **cnāwan**, *to know*	**cnēow**	**cnēowon**	**gecnāwen**
(*e*) **grōwan**, *to grow*	**grēow**	**grēowon**	**gegrōwen**
(*f*) **wēpan**, *to weep*	**wēop**	**wēopon**	**gewōpen**

Like **healdan** go **fealdan**, *to fold;* **feallan**, *to fall;* **wealcan**, *to roll;* **wealdan**, *to wield;* **weallan**, *to boil;* and **weaxan**, *to grow* (originally belonging to class VI).

Like **spannan** go **gangan**, *to go* (pret. also **gīeng**, **gēng**), and **bannan**, *to summon* (pret. also **bēnn**).

Like **bēatan** go **hēawan**, *to hew;* and **hlēapan**, *to run.*

Like **cnāwan** go **blāwan**, *to blow;* **crāwan**, *to crow;* **māwan**, *to mow;* **sāwan**, *to sow;* **wāwan**, *to blow,* and **swāpan**, *to sweep.*

Like **grōwan** go **blōtan**, *to sacrifice;* **blōwan**, *to blossom;* **flōwan**, *to flow;* **hrōpan**, *to shout;* **hwōpan**, *to threaten;* **rōwan**, *to row;* **spōwan**, *to succeed;* **swōgan**, *to sound;* and a few others.

The **ē** in **wēpan** results from front mutation (§§ 39, 160).

WEAK VERBS

191. There are three conjugations in Old English. Only four Old English verbs belong to weak class III, and these are best regarded as irregular verbs. Verbs of class II may be recognized by the ending **-ian** of the infinitive and, as a rule, by the absence of front mutation of the stem-vowel. All verbs of class I show front mutation of the stem-vowel and most of them have the ending **-an** in the infinitive, but a few verbs, especially those whose stems end in **r** in Old English, have the ending **-ian** (§ 193).

192. Verbs of this conjugation may be divided into three groups :

(*a*) Verbs which show front mutation throughout the conjugation and whose stems in primitive Germanic consisted of a short monosyllable.

(*b*) Verbs which show front mutation throughout the conjugation and whose stems in primitive Germanic consisted of a long monosyllable or more than one syllable.

(*c*) Verbs which show front mutation in the present but not in the preterite or past participle.

193. DIVISION (*a*)

PRESENT

Indicative

Sing.	1.	**nerie,** *I save*	**fremme,** *I perform*	**sette,** *I set*
	2.	**neres(t)**	**fremes(t)**	**setst**
	3.	**nereþ**	**fremeþ**	**set(t)**
Pl.		**neriaþ**	**fremmaþ**	**settaþ**

Subjunctive

Sing.	**nerie**	**fremme**	**sette**
Pl.	**nerien**	**fremmen**	**setten**

Imperative

Sing.	2.	**nere**	**freme**	**sete**
Pl.	2.	**neriaþ**	**fremmaþ**	**settaþ**

Infinitive

nerian	**fremman**	**settan**

Participle

neriende	**fremmende**	**settende**

PRETERITE

Indicative

Sing.	1.	**nerede**	**fremede**	**sette**
	2.	**neredes(t)**	**fremedes(t)**	**settes(t)**
	3.	**nerede**	**fremede**	**sette**
Pl.		**neredon**	**fremedon**	**setton**

Subjunctive

| Sing. | nerede | **fremede** | sette |
| Pl. | nereden | **fremeden** | setten |

Participle

| | genered | **gefremed** | geseted, geset(t) |

Like **nerian** are conjugated **andswerian,** *to answer;* **derian,** *to injure;* **spyrian,** *to follow;* and a few other verbs. Because of the similarity of ending in the infinitive, verbs of this type tend to pass into class II.

Like **fremman** are conjugated **dynnan,** *to make a noise;* **temman,** *to tame;* **trymman,** *to strengthen;* and a few others. Because of the similarity of the preterite endings, verbs of this type sometimes adopt infinitives with a single medial consonant and with the ending **-ian,** after the pattern of **nerian,** as **temian, trymian.** On the other hand, the double consonant of the infinitive is sometimes extended to the pret. and pp., as in **getrymmed** beside **getrymed.**

Like **settan** are conjugated verbs with medial **-dd-** or **-tt-,** as **hwettan,** *to incite;* **āhreddan,** *to rescue.*

One verb in **cg** also belongs here, **lecgan,** *to lay.*

Note.—In verbs of the **nerian** type the spellings **g, ig,** and **ige** sometimes occur for **i,** as in **nergan, nerigan, nerigean.**

194. DIVISION (*b*)

PRESENT

Indicative

Sing. 1.	dēme,	drence,	hyngre,	gierwe,
	I judge	*I give to drink*	*I am hungry*	*I prepare*
2.	dēm(e)st	drenc(e)st	hyngrest	gierest
3.	dēm(e)þ	drenc(e)þ	hyngreþ	giereþ
Pl.	dēmaþ	drencaþ	hyngraþ	gierwaþ

Subjunctive

| Sing. | dēme | drence | hyngre | gierwe |
| Pl. | dēmen | drencen | hyngren | gierwen |

Imperative

| Sing. 2. | dēm | drenc | hyngre | giere |
| Pl. 2. | dēmaþ | drencaþ | hyngraþ | gierwaþ |

Infinitive

| dēman | drencan | hyngran | gierwan |

Participle

| dēmende | drencende | hyngrende | gierwende |

PRETERITE

Indicative

		dēman	drencan	hyngran	gierwan
Sing.	1.	dēmde	drencte	hyngrede	gierede
	2.	dēmdes(t)	drenctes(t)	hyngredes(t)	gieredes(t)
	3.	dēmde	drencte	hyngrede	gierede
Pl.		dēmdon	drencton	hyngredon	gieredon

Subjunctive

| Sing. | dēmde | drencte | hyngrede | gierede |
| Pl. | dēmden | drencten | hyngreden | giereden |

Participle

| gedēmed | gedrenced | gehyngred | gegier(w)ed |

Like **dēman** are conjugated many verbs whose stems end in a voiced consonant, as **fēdan,** *to feed;* **lǣran,** *to teach;* **wēnan,** *to expect.*

Like **drencan** are conjugated many verbs whose stems end in a voiceless consonant, as **bētan,** *to make amends;* **scencan,** *to pour out.*

Like **hyngran** are conjugated verbs with stems ending in a consonant followed by a liquid or nasal, as **timbran,** *to build;* **seglan, siglan,** *to sail.* Verbs of this type often pass into class II.

Like **gierwan** are conjugated a few verbs with stems ending in **rw, as besierwan,** *to lie in wait for.*

Note 1.—Verbs with stems ending in **þ** generally show assimilation of **þd** to **dd** in the preterite (§ 90), as **cȳþan,** *to make known,* pret. **cȳdde.**

Note 2.—Verbs with stems ending in a double consonant or in a consonant followed by **d** or **t** show simplification in the preterite (§ 101), as **fyllan,** *to fill,* pret. **fylde; cyssan,** *to kiss,* pret. **cyste;** and **wyrdan,** *to answer,* pret. **andwyrde; gelǣstan,** *to carry out,* pret. **gelǣste.**

Note 3.—Verbs like **hyngran** have **e** in the imperative singular and preterite although the stem is long (§ 72).

Note 4.—On the loss of **w** before **i** in the 2 and 3 sing. pres. ind., imper. sing. and pret. of **gierwan** see § 93.

Note 5.—A few contracted verbs belong to this conjugation, as **hēan,** *to exalt,* pret. **hēade,** pp. **gehēad; pȳn,** *to press,* pret. **pȳde,** pp. **gepȳd.**

Note 6.—Verbs with medial **c** often formed the pret. in **-hte** and the pp. in **-ht** on the analogy of Division (*c*). Examples are **bepǣcan**, *to deceive*, **bepǣhte**, **bepǣht**; **īecan**, *to increase*, **īhte** (beside **īecte**), **geīht**.

195.   DIVISION (*c*)

About twenty verbs belonging to weak class I formed their pret. and pp. already in primitive Germanic without the medial vowel **-i-**. These verbs show front mutation in the present but not in the preterite or past participle. Verbs of this type with stems ending in a palatal consonant or a palatal group of consonants have **ht** in the preterite and past participle.

bringan, *to bring*	**brōhte**	**gebrōht**
bycgan, *to buy*	**bohte**	**geboht**
cweccan, *to shake*	**cweahte**	**gecweaht**
rǣcan, *to reach*	**rǣhte**, **rāhte**	**gerǣht**
sēcan, *to seek*	**sōhte**	**gesōht**
sellan, *to give*	**sealde**	**geseald**
þencan, *to think*	**pōhte**	**geþōht**
þyncan, *to seem*	**pūhte**	**geþūht**
wyrcan, *to work*	**worhte**	**geworht**

Like **cweccan** go **dreccan**, *to afflict;* **leccan**, *to moisten;* **reccan**, *to narrate;* **streccan**, *to stretch;* **þeccan**, *to cover;* **weccan**, *to awake.* Like **rǣcan** goes **tǣcan**, *to teach.* Like **sellan** go **cwellan**, *to kill;* **dwellan**, *to hinder;* **stellan**, *to place;* **tellan**, *to count.*

Note 1.—On the loss of **n** in the preterites **brōhte**, **pōhte**, **pūhte** and on the ō in **brōhte**, **pōhte** see § 21. The infinitive which corresponds to **brōhte** is **brengan**, which is rare in Old English ; **bringan** is a related strong verb of class III with a rare pp. **gebrungen**. On the interchange between **y** and **o** in **bycgan** and **wyrcan** see § 42.

Note 2.—**rǣcan**, **tǣcan** generally had preterite **rǣhte**, **tǣhte**, with **ǣ** from the present, beside **rāhte**, **tāhte**. Similarly in late Old English, verbs with **-ecc-** generally had preterites with **e** from the present instead of **ea**. Beside **sellan** there occurs in late West Saxon **syllan** by a sound-change which caused the group **sel-** to become **syl-**. In some non-WS. dialects the group became **sil-**, as in **sillan**.

Note 3.—In late Old English, verbs with **-ell-** sometimes formed the preterite and past participle on the analogy of verbs like **fremman** (§ 193) and, like them, sometimes passed into class II. For example, we find **dwelede**, **dwelode** beside **dwealde**, pret. of **dwellan**.

CLASS II

196. This class, which is a very large one, consists for the most part of verbs formed from nouns or adjectives by the addition of an ending which appears in Old English as **-ian**. On the absence of front mutation in verbs of this class see § 43.

PRESENT

		Indicative	Subjunctive	Imperative
Sing.	1.	lufie, *I love*	lufie	
	2.	lufast	lufie	lufa
	3.	lufaþ	lufie	
Pl.		lufiaþ	lufien	lufiaþ

Infinitive : **lufian**
Present Participle : **lufiende**

PRETERITE

		Indicative	Subjunctive
Sing.	1.	lufode	lufode
	2.	lufodest	lufode
	3.	lufode	lufode
Pl.		lufodon	lufoden

Past Participle : **gelufod**

Like **lufian** are conjugated **bodian,** *to proclaim;* **eardian,** *to inhabit;* **leornian,** *to learn,* and many others.

Note.—In the pret. the medial vowel appears as **u** in the oldest texts and as **a** in most non-West Saxon texts, as in **lufude, lufade** beside **lufode.** In the pret. ind. pl. the medial **o** often becomes **e** by dissimilation before the back vowel of the ending (§ 73).

CLASS III

197.   PRESENT

	Indicative			
Sing. 1.	hæbbe, *I have*	libbe, *I live*	secge, *I say*	hycge, *I think*
2.	hafas(t), hæfst	liofas(t)	sagas(t), sægst, segest	hogas(t), hyg(e)st

Indicative (*Contd.*)

	3. hafaþ, hæfþ	liofaþ	sagaþ, sægþ, hogaþ, segeþ	hyg(e)þ
Pl.	habbaþ	libbaþ	secg(e)aþ	hycg(e)aþ

Subjunctive

Sing.	hæbbe	libbe	secge	hycge
Pl.	hæbben	libben	secgen	hycgen

Imperative

Sing. 2.	hafa	liofa	saga, sæge, sege	hoga, hyge
Pl. 2.	habbaþ	libbaþ	secg(e)aþ	hycg(e)aþ

Infinitive

habban	libban	secg(e)an	hycg(e)an

Participle

hæbbende	libbende	secgende	hycgende

PRETERITE

Indicative

Sing. 1.	hæfde	lifde	sægde	hogde
2.	hæfdes(t)	lifdes(t)	sægdes(t)	hogdes(t)
3.	hæfde	lifde	sægde	hogde
Pl.	hæfdon	lifdon	sægdon	hogdon

Subjunctive

Sing.	hæfde	lifde	sægde	hogde
Pl.	hæfden	lifden	sægden	hogden

Participle

gehæfd	gelifd	gesægd	gehogod

Note 1.—The forms with **æ** before **bb** in the present of **habban** are due to the borrowing of **a** from such forms as **habban, hafast, hafaþ** after the time of fronting but before the time of front mutation (cf. § 41(*a*)).

Note 2.—The forms with **io** in the conjugation of **libban** are due to back mutation (§ 45). Beside **libban** there occurred **lifian, leofian,** common in Anglian and Kentish and conjugated like **lufian** (§ 196.)

Note 3.—**segest, segeþ, sege** are late formations on the analogy of verbs of weak class I, such as **lecgan**, *to lay*. In the preterite of **secgan** there occur forms like **sǣde** beside **sægde** (§ 99).

Note 4.—On the interchange of **o** and **y** in the conjugation of **hycgan** see § 42. In the pret. this verb was also inflected like class II, **hogode**, etc., and the pp. **gehogod** is formed after the pattern of that class.

PRETERITE-PRESENT VERBS

198. These are strong verbs of which the preterite forms gained a present meaning and for which new weak preterites were made in primitive Germanic. By a shift of emphasis the preterite of one verb came to be regarded as the present of another verb of slightly different meaning. For example, **wāt**, *I know*, is derived from the old perfect of a verb meaning *to see* and is cognate with Latin **vidēre**. The preterites and past participles of preterite-present verbs were formed like those of division (*c*) of weak class I (§ 195). As a result of consonant-changes taking place in primitive Germanic, verbs with present stems ending in **g** have **ht** and those with stems ending in **t** have **ss** (or, by analogy, **st**) in the pret. and in the 2 sing. pres. ind.

199. In two respects preterite-present verbs preserve older features of the Germanic system which have been replaced by analogical forms in other classes of verbs :

(*a*) The 2 sing. pres. ind. preserves the early method of forming the 2 sing. pret. by the addition of **t** to the stem of the first and third persons, as in **scealt.** Some preterite-present verbs have the ending **-st** in the 2 sing. pres. ind., as **canst** (§ 203), **manst** (§ 207), **āhst** (§ 210). This ending is probably due to the analogy of the ending **-st** found in strong and weak verbs.

(*b*) Subjunctive forms sometimes show front mutation. The forms with front mutation, such as **dyge** (§ 201), **þyrfe** (§ 204), **dyrre** (§ 205), are older but less frequent than the forms without front mutation, **duge, þurfe, durre.**

The following verbs, many of which are defective, are the Old English preterite-present verbs. The endings of the pres. subj. and pret. ind. and subj. forms, so far as they are recorded, are the same as those of **dēman** (§ 194).

200.   CLASS I

wāt, *I know*

Pres. Ind. 1, 3 Sing.	wāt;	2 Sing.	wāst;	Pl.	witon
Pres. Subj.	wite;	Imper. Sing.	wite;	Pl.	witaþ
Infin.	witan;	Pres. Part.	witende		
Pret.	wisse,	Past Part.	gewiten		
	wiste;				

Participial Adj. gewiss, *certain*

Note 1.—In the pres. ind. pl. and infin. the i of the stem sometimes becomes io or eo by back mutation (§ 45). Other forms of the pres. ind. pl. are **wuton** (§ 48), and **wieton** (§ 10).

Note 2.—On negative forms like **nāt**, *I do not know*, see § 94.

201.   CLASS II

dēag, *I avail*

Pres. Ind. 1, 3 Sing.	dēag, dēah;	Pl. dugon
Pres. Subj.	dyge, duge;	Infin. dugan
Pres. Part.	dugende;	Pret. dohte

202.   CLASS III

ann, *I grant*

Pres. Ind. 1, 3 Sing.	an(n), on(n);	Pl.	unnon
Pres. Subj.	unne;	Imper. Sing.	unne
Infin.	unnan;	Pres. Part.	unnende
Pret.	ūþe;	Past. Part.	geunnen

203.   cann, *I know, can*

Pres. Ind. 1, 3 Sing.	can(n),	2 Sing. canst;	Pl. cunnon
	con(n);		
Pres. Subj.	cunne;	Infin.	cunnan
Pret.	cūþe;	Past. Part.	-cunnen

Participial Adj. cūþ, *known*

204.   þearf, *I need*

Pres. Ind.

1, 3 Sing.	þearf;	2 Sing. þearft;	Pl.	þurfon
Pres. Subj.	þyrfe, þurfe;		Infin.	þurfan
Pres. Part.	þurfende;	Participial Adj. þearfende, *needy*		
Pret.	þorfte			

Note.—There is a variant form of the present participle **þyrfende** with **y** from the subj. The participial adj. **þearfende** has **ea** from the pres. ind. sing.

205.   **dearr,** *I dare*

Pres. Ind.

  1, 3 Sing. **dear(r);**   2 Sing. **dearst;**   Pl.   **durron**

Pres. Subj. **dyrre, durre;**   Pret. **dorste**

Note.—The stem of this verb ended in **-rs** (cf. Gothic **gadars**). In the plural **rs** became **rz** by Verner's Law (§ 77) and the **z** became **r** in West Germanic (§ 79). From the plural, **rr** spread to the 1 and 3 sing. pres. ind.

206.   CLASS IV

                   sceal, *I shall, must*

Pres. Ind.

  1, 3 Sing. **sceal;**   2 Sing. **scealt;**   Pl.   **sculon,**
                                             sc(e)olon

Pres. Subj. **scyle, scule,**   Infin. **sculan,**
            sc(e)ole ;   **sc(e)olan**

Pret.   **sc(e)olde**

Note.—On forms with **e** after **sc** see § 9.

207. man, *I think;* **geman,** *I remember;* **onman,** *I esteem.*

Pres. Ind.

  1, 3 Sing. **man, mon;**   2 Sing. **manst, monst;** Pl. **munon**

Pres. Subj. **myne, mune;**   Imper. Sing. **-mun, -myne, -mune**

Infin.   **munan;**   Pres. Part.   **munende**

Pret.   **munde;**   Past. Part.   **gemunen**

208.   **beneah, geneah,** *it suffices*

Pres. Ind. Sing **-neah;**   Pl.   **-nugon**

Pres. Subj.   **-nuge;**   Pret. **-nohte**

209.   CLASS VI

                   mōt, *I may*

Pres. Ind. 1, 3 Sing. **mōt;**   2 Sing. **mōst;**   Pl.   **mōton**

Pres. Subj.   **mōte;**   Infin.   **mōtan**

Pret.   **mōste;**

210. Two preterite-present verbs do not correspond exactly with any of the classes of strong verbs. The verb **āg,** *I have,* resembles verbs of class I, but the **ā** of the sing. has been

extended by analogy throughout the conjugation of the verb.
Similarly **mæg**, *I am able*, may belong to strong class V, but
the vowel of the pres. ind. sing. has been extended throughout
the conjugation.

āg, *I have*

Pres. Ind.

1, 3 Sing.	**āg, āh;**	2 Sing. **āhst;**	Pl.		**āgon**
Pres. Subj.	**āge;**	Imper. **āge;**	Infin.		**āgan**
Pret.	**āhte;**		Past Part.		**āgen, ǣgen**

211.   **mæg**, *I am able*

Pres. Ind.

1, 3 Sing.	**mæg;**	2 Sing. **meaht, miht;**	Pl.	**magon**
Pres Subj.	**mæge;**		Infin.	**magan**
Pres. Part.	**magende;**	Pret. **meahte, mihte, mehte**		

       Participial Adj. **meaht, miht,** *mighty*

Note.—Preterites with **ea** are indicative forms ; those with **i** are from
the subjunctive with front mutation (§ 39). Forms with **e** are
late West Saxon (§ 53).

VERBS IN -mi

212. The first person singular present indicative of the
Indo-European verb ended in either **-ō** or **-mi**, and the two
endings are preserved in different classes of Greek verbs.
The vast majority of Old English verbs belong to the **-ō** class.
Only four Old English verbs belong to the **-mi** class, but they
are very commonly used ; that is no doubt the reason why
they were able to preserve their irregularities of conjugation.
They are : **eom**, *I am;* **dōn**, *to do;* **gān**, *to go;* **willan**, *to wish,
be willing.*

THE SUBSTANTIVE VERB

213. The full conjugation of the verb ' to be ' is made
up from three distinct roots : (*a*) **es-, er-** (cf. Latin **esse**),
(*b*) **bheu-** (cf. Latin. **fui**), (*c*) **wes-**, which gave rise to **wesan,**
a strong verb of class V which has supplied all the preterite
forms of the verb ' to be ' and some of the present forms.

Present Indicative

Sing.	1.	**eom**	**bēo**
	2.	**eart**	**bist**
	3.	**is**	**biþ**
Pl.		**sint, sindon**	**bēoþ, bīoþ**

Present Subjunctive

Sing.	sīe	bēo, bīo	
Pl.	sīen	bēon, bīon	
Imper. Sing.		bēo	wes
Pl.		bēoþ	wesaþ
Infin.		bēon	wesan
Pres. Part		bēonde	wesende

Pret. Ind. 1, 3 Sing. **wæs**; 2 Sing. **wǣre**; Pl. **wǣron**

Pret. Subj. Sing. **wǣre**; Pl. **wǣren**

Note 1.—Anglian forms of the present indicative are : 1 sing. **eam, am, bīom**; 2 sing. **earþ, arþ**; pl. **earon, aron, bi(o)þun**.

Note 2.—Negative forms occur with contraction of the negative particle **ne** with verbal forms, as **nis, næs, nǣron** (§ 94).

214. dōn, *to do*

	Indicative	Subjunctive	Imperative
Sing. 1.	dō	dō	
2.	dēst	dō	dō
3.	dēþ	dō	
Pl.	dōþ	dōn	dōþ
Infin.	dōn;	Pres. Part. **dōnde**	

PRETERITE

	Indicative	Subjunctive
Sing. 1.	dyde	dyde
2.	dydes(t)	dyde
3.	dyde	dyde
Pl.	dydon	dyden
Past. Part. **gedōn**		

Note.—Anglian forms of the present indicative are : 1 sing. **dōm, dōam**; 2 sing. **dōes(t), dōas**; 3 sing. **dōeþ, dōas**; pl. **dōaþ, dōas**. Kentish has a pret. sing. **dede**, pl. **deodon**.

215. gān, *to go*

PRESENT

	Indicative	Subjunctive	Imperative
Sing. 1.	gā	gā	
2.	gǣst	gā	gā
3.	gǣþ	gā	
Pl.	gāþ	gān	gāþ
	Infin. **gān**;	Past. Part. **gegān**	

The preterite indicative and subjunctive are supplied from a different verb : 1, 3 sing. ind. **ēode,** 2 sing. **ēodest,** pl. **ēodon;** subj. sing. **ēode,** pl. **ēoden.**

216. **willan,** *to wish, be willing*

	Indicative	Subjunctive
Sing. 1.	**wille**	**wil(l)e**
2.	**wilt**	**wil(l)e**
3.	**wil(l)e**	**wil(l)e**
Pl.	**willaþ**	**willen**

Infin. **willan;** Pres. Part. **willende**

PRETERITE

	Indicative	Subjunctive
Sing. 1.	**wolde**	**wolde**
2.	**woldest**	**wolde**
3.	**wolde**	**wolde**
Pl.	**woldon**	**wolden**

Note 1.—The 1 sing. pres. ind. **wille** (cf. Gothic **wiljáu**) and the 3 sing. **wile** (cf. Gothic **wili**) are old subjunctive forms ; the 3 sing. **wille** is due to confusion with the 1 sing.

Note 2.—Negative forms frequently occur showing contraction of the negative particle **ne** with the verb, as **nolde,** *would not* (§ 94). In the present tense, the negative forms generally have **y** in early West Saxon (§ 58) but **e** in late West Saxon. Examples are : 1 sing. pres. ind. **nylle, nelle;** 3 sing. **nyle, nele;** pl. **nyllaþ, nellaþ.**

CHAPTER VIII

SYNTAX

217. In many respects the syntax of Old English is similar to that of Modern English. The object of the present chapter is not to give a complete survey of Old English syntax but to call attention to such differences between the syntax of Old English and that of Modern English as are likely to cause difficulty to a student reading Old English texts.

WORD-ORDER

218. The order of words is less rigid in Old English than in Modern English because the Old English inflectional system, much fuller than that of Modern English, made it possible for a writer to make clear the relation of a word to the rest of the sentence without making use of word-order for this purpose.

A title used in apposition to a proper name without a definite article generally follows the name : **Ælfred kyning,** *King Alfred;* **Wærferð biscep,** *Bishop Wœrferð.* A noun qualified by the genitive of such a group is usually placed between the name and the title : **on Herōdes dagum cyninges,** *in the days of King Herod.*

An adjective usually precedes the noun which it qualifies, but when it is used with the definite article the adjective often follows the noun : **ēce Dryhten,** *eternal Lord,* beside **Ēadweard sē langa,** *the tall Edward.*

An auxiliary verb is often separated by a number of words from the infinitive or participle that belongs with it, **hīe ne dorston forþ bi þǣre ēa siglan,** *they dared not sail beyond the river.*

When a sentence begins with the demonstrative adverb **þā** it is usual for a verb to precede its subject : **þā ongeat sē cyning þæt,** *then the king perceived that.*

In a dependent clause the verb is usually put at the end : **hī wǣron þæs Hǣlendes gewitan, ðēah ðe hī hine ðā gȳt ne cūðon,** *they were witnesses of the Saviour although they did not yet know Him.* The verb is similarly often put at the end of co-ordinate clauses joined together by **and: ond hī ðonne**

fullfremeð, ond hī him ðonne fullīce līciað, and hē hī nǣfre
forlǣtan ne ðencð, *and (he) then completes them, and they please
him very much, and he never thinks of leaving them.*

Words which logically belong together are often separated
from each other for stylistic reasons, especially in poetry.
A common cause of this separation is the desire to emphasize
one of the words : ǣr-ðǣm-ðe hit eall forhergod wǣre ond
forbærned, *before it was all ravaged and burnt up;* hē lēt
him þā of handon lēofne flēogan hafoc wið þæs holtes, *he
allowed his beloved hawk to fly from his hands towards the wood.*

APPOSITION

219. Apposition is used more freely in Old English than it
is today ; it is especially common in Old English poetry.
Corresponding to the Modern English *the island of Britain,*
Old English had **Breten īegland,** where the two nouns are in
apposition and are declined separately.

Corresponding to the Modern English *some of,* where *some*
is pronominal, Old English has the adjective **sum** with a noun
or pronoun in apposition, as þā tēð hīe brōhton sume þǣm
cyninge, *they brought some of the teeth to the king.*

Adjectives in **-weard** agree with the noun where Modern
English has the partitive genitive (cf. Latin **summus mons,**
the top of the mountain) : tōemnes þǣm lande sūðeweardum,
alongside the southern part of the land.

CORRELATION

220. Correlation is generally expressed more fully in Old
English than in Modern English : ðā ic ðā ðis eall gemunde,
ðā gemunde ic ēac, *when I remembered all this, (then) I remembered also.*   In ðā ðā, *when,* and ðǣr ðǣr, *where,* the two cor-
relatives are placed together : ðā ðā ic tō rīce fēng, *when I
came to the throne;* ðǣr ðǣr ðū hiene befæstan mæge, *where
you can apply it.*   Sometimes ðā is used in place of ðā ðā, and
ðǣr in place of ðǣr ðǣr : þā hē tō wǣpnum fēng, *when he
took up weapons;* þǣr sē cyning ofslǣgen læg, *where the king
lay slain.*

CONCORD

221. Collective nouns may take a verb either in the
singular or the plural.   When the verb is near to its subject

it is usually singular, but when it is separated from it, especially in co-ordinating clauses, it is often plural : **ðā forrād siō fierd hīe foran . . . ond þā here-hȳþa āhreddon,** *then the army cut them off . . . and recovered the booty.*

A verb with a compound subject is often put in the singular, in agreement with the nearest noun : **Cynewulf benam Sigebryht his rīces ond West-seaxna wiotan,** *Cynewulf and the councillors of the West Saxons deprived Sigebryht of his kingdom.*

When a plural subject follows its verb, the verb is often, but not invariably, in the singular : **hwǣr cwōm symbla gesetu ?,** *where are the banqueting-halls ?* beside **hwǣr sindon seledrēamas ?,** *where are the festivities ?*

The demonstrative pronoun **þæt** is often connected with a plural predicate by a plural form of the verb ' to be ' : **þæt wǣron þā ǣrestan scipu Deniscra manna þe Angelcynnes land gesōhton,** *those were the first ships of the Danes which came to the land of the English people;* **þæt wǣron eall Finnas,** *they were all Finns.*

Expressions of the type **gehwylc þāra þe,** *each of those who,* take a singular verb, agreeing with ' each ', whereas in Modern English we should have a plural verb, agreeing with ' those ', as **ðās lēasan spell lǣrað gehwylcne monn ðāra ðe wilnað helle ðiostro tō flīonne,** *these false stories teach everyone of those who wish to flee from the darkness of Hell.*

When participles are used as adjectives they agree with the noun they qualify : **ðā ciricean stōdon māðma ond bōca gefylda,** *the churches stood filled with treasures and books.*

NEGATION

222. The negative particle, **ne,** occurs as a separate word and also contracted with verbs and pronouns, as **nyllan,** *to be unwilling,* from **ne willan; nān,** *no,* from **ne ān** (§ 94). **Ne . . . ne** is used with the sense *neither . . . nor.* Two or more negatives are often used in the same sentence in order to strengthen the negation ; they do not make an affirmative : **nān heort ne onscunode nǣnne lēon, ne nān hara nǣnne hund, ne nān nēat nyste nǣnne andan ne nǣnne ege tō ōðrum,** *no hart was afraid of any lion, nor any hare of any hound, and no animal knew any hatred or fear of another.*

CASES

Nominative

223. The nominative is used for the subject of a sentence and for words in apposition to the subject : **wæs hē, sē mon, in weoruldhāde geseted,** *this man was a layman.*

It is used to express the vocative, which does not survive as a separate case in Old English : **gehȳrst þū, sǣlida?** *do you hear, seafarer?*

Accusative

224. The accusative is used primarily as the direct object of a verb : **hīe begēaton welan,** *they obtained wealth.*

It is used adverbially to denote extent of time or space : **ealne weg,** *all the way, always;* **þæt is tū hund mīla brād,** *it is two hundred miles broad.*

It is used with some impersonal verbs : **hine nānes ðinges ne lyste,** *nothing pleased him.*

It is used after many prepositions : **geond ealne ymbhwyrft,** *throughout all the world.*

Genitive

225. The genitive usually expresses the relation between one noun and another. The most common relation is the possessive, as in **þæs cyninges þegnas,** *the king's thanes;* but a noun in the genitive is sometimes used as the complement of another noun to define or describe it : **þā betstan meregrotan ǣlces hīwes,** *the best pearls of every colour.*

It is often used in a partitive sense : **þāra wǣron syx stælhrānas,** *six of them were decoy reindeer;* **hē syxa sum,** *he in a party of six.*

It is used with many verbs, especially those which denote mental action : **ne brēac sē ārlēasa Herōdes his cynerīces,** *the cruel Herod did not enjoy his kingdom.* It is also used with verbs of depriving to denote the object withheld : **Cynewulf benam Sigebryht his rīces,** *Cynewulf deprived Sigebryht of his kingdom.*

It is used with certain prepositions, most of which also govern other cases : **tō hwilces tīman,** *at what time ;* **wið Exanceastres,** *against Exeter.*

It is used as the complement of an adjective : **earfeþa gemyndig,** *mindful of hardships.*

4

Nouns in the genitive are sometimes used adverbially, as **nihtes,** *by night;* **dæges,** *by day;* **ealles,** *altogether* (§ 113, Note 2).

Dative

226. The dative has two chief functions : to represent the indirect object of a verb and to replace the instrumental, originally a separate case, of which a few survivals remain in Old English, notably in the demonstrative pronoun (§ 138). The dative usually indicates personal relations, and many verbs take an accusative of the thing and a dative of the person : **sing mē hwæthwegu,** *sing me something.*

The dative is used with many verbs, especially those of giving, addressing, and obeying : **ic ēow secge,** *I say to you ;* **ðā kyningas Gode ond his ǣrendwrecum hȳrsumedon,** *the kings obeyed God and his messengers.*

It is used to denote the person indirectly affected or benefited, as **Burgenda land wæs ūs on bæcbord,** *Bornholm was on our port side;* **þām þe him lȳt hafað lēofra geholena,** *to him who has few beloved protectors (for himself).* This use of the dative is sometimes closely akin to the possessive : **hē sette his hond him on þæt hēafod,** *he laid his hand on his head.*

It is frequently used with impersonal verbs : **wæs him geþūht,** *it seemed to him.*

It is by far the most common case after prepositions, as **on dēora fellum,** *in deer-skins.* The preposition **tō** is often used with a noun in the dative to indicate purpose or function : **ūs tō woruldscame,** *as a great shame to us;* **tō gefēran,** *as a companion.*

A noun in the dative and a participle in agreement with it are sometimes used absolutely, like the Latin ablative absolute, as the equivalent of an adverbial clause, usually one of time : **him sprecendum, hig cōmon,** *while he was speaking, they came.*

The dative is used to form adverbs or adverbial phrases of time or manner : **sumre tīde,** *at a certain time;* **wundrum,** *wondrously.*

It is used to denote the instrument or manner of an action, as **hē hlūtre mōde and bylewite and smyltre willsumnesse Dryhtne þēowde,** *he served God with a pure and innocent heart and with gentle willingness.*

ADJECTIVES

227. The weak forms (§ 122) are used :

(*a*) after the definite article : **sē swicola Herōdes,** *the deceitful Herod;* **hīo geseah þone fordrifenan cyning,** *she saw the king* (*who had been*) *driven out of his course ;*

(*b*) after the demonstrative adjective **þes: on þisse earman forsyngodan þēode,** *in this miserable sinful people;*

(*c*) often after possessive adjectives : **mīn lēofa sunu,** *my dear son;*

(*d*) usually in vocative phrases : **lēofan menn,** *beloved men* (the opening of a sermon) ;

(*e*) often in poetry : **sweotolan tācne,** *by a clear sign* (*Beowulf,* l. 141).

The adjectives **eall,** *all;* **fēawe,** *few;* **genōg,** *enough;* **manig,** *many;* **ōþer,** *second;* and possessive adjectives like **mīn,** *my,* are always declined according to the strong declension. The adjective **ilca,** *same,* ordinal numerals except **ōþer,** and comparatives and superlatives (except the nom. and acc. sing. neuter in **-est, -ost**) are always declined according to the weak declension. **ān** in the sense of *one* has the strong form to distinguish it from the weak form **āna,** which means *alone.*

228. The noun qualified by an adjective is often not expressed but left to be understood, as (in poetry) **dōmgeorne drēorigne oft in hyra brēostcofan bindað fæste,** *those eager for glory often bind fast in their hearts a sad thought.* Hence adjectives come to be used as nouns : **hōcorwyrde dysige,** *derisive foolish* (*ones*), i.e. *foolish deriders.*

ARTICLES

229. The definite article is often omitted : **hē wolde gesēcan helle godu,** *he wished to seek the gods of the underworld.* The omission of the definite article is especially common after prepositions : **ic tō rīce fēng,** *I came to the throne.*

When a noun in the genitive is dependent on another noun, we sometimes find that each noun is accompanied by a definite article, as in Modern English, as **for ðǣre mergðe ðæs sōnes,** *because of the joy caused by the music,* but it is more common to find only one definite article, agreeing in the genitive wish the dependent noun, which immediately precedes the main noun, as **ðǣre helle hund,** *the hound of the underworld;* **þæs cyninges þegnas,** *the king's thanes;* **þæs landes scēawung,** *the exploration of the land.*

The definite article is used with proper names to indicate that the name has been mentioned before, as **sē Cynewulf,** *this Cynewulf;* **sē Cyneheard,** *this Cyneheard.*

The indefinite article is sometimes expressed by **ān,** from which the Modern English indefinite article is derived, as **ān micel ēa,** *a great river.* Sometimes it is expressed by **sum,** as **sum mann,** *a (certain) man.* It is often not expressed at all, as **ic wāt þæt þū eart heard mann,** *I know that you are a hard man.*

PRONOUNS

230. The genitive of the personal pronoun in Old English is not a mere possessive adjective ; it may be a partitive genitive or the object of a verb which takes the genitive, as **eal þæt his man āðer oðð ettan oðð erian mæg,** *all of it that can be either grazed or ploughed;* **God ūre helpe,** *God help us.*

Nouns are often qualified by both the definite article and the genitive case of a personal pronoun : **sette his þā swīðran hond him on þæt hēafod,** *he laid his right hand on his head.*

A relative pronoun is generally represented by the relative particle **þe,** either alone or in combination with the demonstrative or personal pronoun. Since the particle **þe** is indeclinable, the addition of an oblique case of the personal pronoun is the usual way of indicating an oblique case of the relative : **þe his** means *whose,* **þe him,** *to whom,* etc. Examples are : **saga hwæt ic hātte, þe ic lond rēafige,** *say what I am called, I who lay waste the land;* **nis nū cwicra nān þe ic him mōdsefan mīnne durre sweotule āsecgan,** *there is now none of those alive to whom I dare openly express my thoughts.*

In the third person the demonstrative pronoun is used as a relative without the addition of **þe** : **þonne tōdǣlað hī his feoh, þæt þǣr tō lāfe bið,** *then they divide his property which is left there.*

The demonstrative pronoun is sometimes used as an emphatic form of the personal pronoun : **sē swīþe gewundad wæs,** *he was severely wounded.*

Personal pronouns are used to express the reflexive : **sē cyning unhēanlīce hine werede,** *the king defended himself dauntlessly.*

In order to emphasize the personal pronoun, whether it is used reflexively or not, the appropriate case of **self** (declined strong or weak) is added : **hē hit self ne geseah,** *he did not see it himself;* **ic ðā sōna eft mē selfum andwyrde,** *then immediately afterwards I answered myself.*

PREPOSITIONS

231. Prepositions sometimes follow the words they modify, sometimes with other words intervening : **beraŏ mē hwæþere hūsl tō,** *nevertheless bring the Sacrament to me;* **þā stōd him sum monn æt þurh swefn,** *then a man stood before him in a dream.* This word-order is the regular one in subordinate clauses introduced by the relative particle **þe** (§ 230) : **þe hē on būde,** *in which he lived.*

The noun or pronoun modified by a preposition is sometimes not expressed, and the preposition then becomes adverbial : **oŏŏe hwā ōŏre bī wrīte,** *or (unless) someone is making a copy.*

VERBS

Tenses

232. There are no inflectional endings to indicate the future tense in Old English. As a rule the present tense is used for the future: **ic selle ēow þæt riht biþ,** *I will give you what is right.* The future is sometimes expressed by *shall* and *will* as in Modern English, though the auxiliary **willan** generally implies volition and **sculan** implies necessity in addition to the idea of simple futurity : **ic tō ælcum biscepstōle on mīnum rīce wille āne onsendan,** *I wish to send one to each bishopric in my kingdom;* **nelle wē ŏās race nā leng tēon,** *we will not prolong this story;* **þone miclan dōm þe wē ealle tō sculan,** *the great Judgement to which we must all go.*

The preterite is used to express the simple past tense, the past continuous, and the perfect ; **hē sægde,** *he said;* **hē wæs swȳŏe spēdig man,** *he was a very wealthy man;* **fæder, ic syngode,** *father, I have sinned.* The preterite is often used to express the pluperfect, and when it is so used it is sometimes strengthened by the addition of the adverb ǣr: þā men þe hē beæftan him lǣfde ǣr, *the men whom he had left behind him.*

Periphrastic tenses are sometimes formed, as in Modern English, by combining parts of the verb **wesan,** *to be,* or **habban,** *to have,* with present or past participles: **he sumu þing ætgædere mid him sprecende and glēowiende wæs,** *he was speaking and joking about some things with them;* **hīe alle on þone cyning wǣrun feohtende,** *they were all fighting against the king.* When a past participle is used with the auxiliary verb **habban** it is sometimes inflected and sometimes not. The use of the inflected form is the older construction and goes back to a time when the participle was regarded not as part of the verb but as an adjective agreeing with the object of **habban.** Inflection of the past participle is especially common when it is preceded by the direct object. Examples are: **oþ þæt hīe hine ofslægenne hæfdon,** *until they had killed him,* beside **wē habbað nū ǣgðer forlǣten ge ðone welan ge ðone wisdōm,** *we have now lost both the wealth and the wisdom.*

sceolde with the infinitive is used as a periphrastic form of the preterite when the writer does not wish to vouch for the truth of the events that he is narrating: **ðā sceolde cuman ðǣre helle hund ongēan hine, þæs nama wæs Cerverus, sē sceolde habban þrīo hēafdu,** (*it is said that*) *the hound of the underworld, whose name was Cerberus, who had three heads, came to meet him.*

Passive

233. Except for the form **hātte** (§ 155) the passive is formed by using **wesan,** *to be,* or **weorþan,** *to become,* with the past participle. The distinction between the two auxiliaries is not always preserved, but in general **wesan** indicates a state, **weorþan** an action: **sē swīþe gewundad wæs,** *he was severely wounded;* **hē wearð ofslægen,** *he was killed.*

Where Modern English has the passive, Old English often has the indefinite pronoun **man,** *one,* with a verb in the active, as **hine man ofslōg,** *one killed him,* i.e. *he was killed.*

Subjunctive

234. The subjunctive is used for statements other than those of fact. It is used in a principal sentence to express a wish or command, usually in the third person: **ābrēoðe his angin!** *may his enterprise fail!*

235. The subjunctive is used in subordinate clauses:

(a) In indirect narrative or question : **hē sǣde þæt þæt land sīe swīþe lang norþ þonan,** *he said that the land extends very far north from there;* **hē frægn hū nēh þǣre tīde wǣre,** *he asked how near to the time it was.* When the statement in the indirect narration is quite certain and is not merely accepted on the authority of the speaker, it is put in the indicative : **ðā gemunde ic hū sīo ǣ wæs ǣrest on Ēbrēisc geðīode funden,** *then I remembered how the law was first found in the Hebrew language.*

(b) After verbs of desiring or commanding : **hīe woldon ðæt hēr ðȳ māra wīsdōm on londe wǣre ðȳ wē mā geðēoda cūðon,** *they wished that there should be the more wisdom here in this land the more languages we knew.*

(c) After verbs of thinking : **ic wēne ðæt nōht monige begiondan Humbre nǣren,** *I think that there were not many beyond the Humber.*

(d) After impersonal verbs expressing necessity or fitness : **nēod is þæt hī bēon efenhlyttan þæs ēcan edlēanes,** *it is necessary that they shall be sharers in the eternal reward.*

(e) To express purpose : **ne cōm hē tō ðȳ þæt hē wǣre on mǣrlicum cynesetle āhafen,** *He did not come in order that he might be exalted on a glorious throne;* **nelle wē ðās race nā leng tēon, þȳ lǣs ðe hit ēow ǣðrȳt þince,** *we will not prolong this narrative, lest it seem tedious to you.*

(f) Sometimes to express result: **þū næfst þā mihte þæt þū mæge him wiþstandan,** *you have not the power to resist him.*

(g) To express hypothetical comparison, generally introduced by **swilce: wildu dīor ðǣr woldon tō irnan ond stondan, swilce hī tamu wǣren,** *wild animals would run there and stand, as though they were tame.*

(h) In conditional clauses, generally introduced by **gif or būtan: ðonne forlȳst hē eall his ǣrran good, būton hē hit eft gebēte,** *then he loses all his former good, unless he afterwards makes atonement for it.* The indicative is sometimes used in conditional clauses : **mē ðyncð betre, gif īow swǣ ðyncð,** *it seems better to me, if it seems so to you.* When the condition is regarded as unreal, both clauses are put in the subjunctive, the preterite being used with reference to the present. The modern distinction between *if he were* and *if he had been* is not made in Old English, which uses **gif hē wǣre** for both :

hit wǣre tō hrǣdlic gif hē ðā on cildcradole ācweald wurde,
*it would have been too early if He had been killed at that time in
the cradle.*

(*i*) In concessive clauses, generally introduced by **þēah**
or **þēah þe: ne forseah Crīst his geongan cempan, ðēah ðe hē
līchamlīce on heora slege andwerd nǣre,** *Christ did not despise
His young champions, although He was not present in person
at their death.*

236. If a clause containing a subjunctive has another
clause dependent on it, the verb in the dependent clause
is put in the subjunctive by attraction. This is the reason
why **tǣcan** is in the subjunctive in the sentence : **þæs ūs
scamað swȳðe þæt wē bōte aginnan, swā swā bēc tǣcan,** *we are
very much ashamed of beginning reform, as the books teach.*
(On the subjunctive in **-an** see § 158.)

237. Sometimes in subordinate clauses **sc(e)olde** or **wolde**
with an infinitive is used in place of the preterite subjunctive:
sc(e)olde is used after verbs of desiring and fearing; **wolde**
after verbs of purpose: **þā wearð hē micclum āfyrht and
anðrācode þæt his rīce feallan sceolde,** *then he was very much
afraid and he feared that his kingdom must fall;* **tō ðȳ hē cōm
þæt hē wolde his heofenlīce rīce gelēaffullum mannum forgyfan,**
*He came in order that He might give His heavenly kingdom to
believers.*

Infinitive

238. An indefinite pronoun is often omitted from the
accusative and infinitive construction after verbs of commanding and hearing. The effect of this omission is to make the
infinitive appear to be passive, as **ðē cȳðan hāte,** *I command
(someone) to make it known to you;* **of þām þe wē nū secgan
hȳrdon,** *of which we have now heard tell.*

The infinitives of verbs of motion and of the verb ' to be '
are often omitted after auxiliary verbs, especially in poetry :
fram ic ne wille, *I will not (run) away;* **wita sceal geþyldig,**
a wise man must be patient.

The inflected form of the infinitive, sometimes called a
gerund (§ 160), is used with the preposition **tō** chiefly to
express purpose and to define an adjective more closely :
ūt ēode sē sāwere his sǣd tō sāwenne, *the sower went out to
sow his seed;* **swā wynsum tō gehȳrenne,** *so pleasant to hear.*

Impersonal Verbs

239. Impersonal verbs are more common in Old English than in Modern English. In Old English the subject 'it' is generally implied, not expressed : **him spēow,** *they succeeded;* **mē ðyncð betre, gif īow swǣ ðyncð,** *it seems better to me if it seems so to you.* Sometimes impersonal verbs take two cases : **ðǣm hearpere ðūhte ðæt hine nānes ðinges ne lyste on ðisse worulde,** *it seemed to the harper that nothing pleased him in this world.*

SELECT BIBLIOGRAPHY

LITERARY BACKGROUND

BATESON, F. W., ed. *The Cambridge Bibliography of English Literature*, 4 vols. Cambridge, 1940. *Supplement*, ed. by George Watson, 1957.

A work of reference which records linguistic studies as well as literary works.

KER, W. P. *The Dark Ages.* Edinburgh, 1923.

KER, W. P. *English Literature Medieval.* Home University Library. London, 1912.

MALONE, KEMP and A. C. BAUGH. *The Middle Ages.* New York, 1948.

The first two parts of *A Literary History of England*, ed. by A. C. Baugh.

RENWICK, W. L. and HAROLD ORTON. *The Beginnings of English Literature to Skelton 1509.* Second edition, London, 1952.

Contains a useful bibliography.

WARDALE, E. E. *Chapters on Old English Literature.* London, 1935.

HISTORICAL BACKGROUND

BLAIR, PETER HUNTER. *An Introduction to Anglo-Saxon England.* Cambridge, 1956.

HODGKIN, R. H. *A History of the Anglo-Saxons*, 2 vols., third edition, with Appendix by R. L. S. Bruce Mitford. Oxford, 1953.

Very well illustrated ; covers the period up to the death of Alfred.

STENTON, Sir FRANK. *Anglo-Saxon England*, second edition. Oxford, 1947.

An authoritative account of the whole Anglo-Saxon period, with full bibliography.

WHITELOCK, DOROTHY. *The Beginnings of English Society.* London, Penguin Books, 1952.

An excellent introduction to the social history of the Anglo-Saxons.

READERS AND BOOKS FOR BEGINNERS

ARDERN, P. S. *First Readings in Old English*, second edition. Wellington, New Zealand, 1951.

COOK, ALBERT S. *A First Book in Old English*, third edition. Boston, 1903.

KRAPP, G. P. and KENNEDY, A. G. *An Anglo-Saxon Reader.* New York, 1930.

MOSSÉ, FERNAND. *Manuel de l'Anglais du Moyen Âge. I Vieil-Anglais. Tome Premier : Grammaire et Textes. Tome Second: Notes et Glossaire. Deuxième Édition.* Paris, 1950.

SEDGEFIELD, W. J. *An Anglo-Saxon Book of Verse and Prose.* Manchester, 1928.

SWEET, HENRY. *Anglo-Saxon Primer*, ninth edition revised by Norman Davis. Oxford, 1953.

SWEET, HENRY. *An Anglo-Saxon Reader*, fourteenth edition, revised by C. T. Onions. Oxford, 1959.

WYATT, ALFRED J. *The Threshold of Anglo-Saxon.* Cambridge, 1926.

WYATT, ALFRED J. *An Anglo-Saxon Reader.* Cambridge, 1919.

GRAMMARS

BRUNNER, KARL. *Altenglische Grammatik nach der angelsächsischen Grammatik von Eduard Sievers*, zweite Auflage. Halle, 1951.

BÜLBRING, KARL D. *Altenglisches Elementarbuch, I teil: Lautlehre.* Heidelberg, 1902.

CAMPBELL, A. *Old English Grammar.* Oxford, 1959.

GIRVAN, RITCHIE. *Angelsaksisch Handboek.* Haarlem, 1931.

LUICK, K. *Historische Grammatik der englischen Sprache.* Leipzig, 1914-39.

QUIRK, RANDOLPH and C. L. WRENN. *An Old English Grammar*, second edition. London, 1958.

WARDALE, E. E. *An Old English Grammar*, third edition. London, 1931.

WRIGHT, J. and E. M. *Old English Grammar*, third edition. Oxford, 1925.

DICTIONARIES

BOSWORTH-TOLLER. *An Anglo-Saxon Dictionary based on the Manuscript Collections of the late Joseph Bosworth.* Edited by T. N. Toller. Oxford, 1882-98. Supplement, 1908-21.

The most complete Anglo-Saxon dictionary, with illustrative quotations.

HALL, JOHN R. CLARK. *A Concise Anglo-Saxon Dictionary*, third edition. Cambridge, 1931.

Gives references to the N.E.D.

HOLTHAUSEN, F. *Altenglisches etymologisches Wörterbuch.* Heidelberg, 1934.

N.E.D. *A New English Dictionary on Historical Principles.* Edited by Sir James Murray, Henry Bradley, Sir William Craigie and C. T. Onions. Oxford, 1888-1933.

Gives the full history of all Old English words which survived in use after the Norman Conquest.

SWEET, HENRY. *The Student's Dictionary of Anglo-Saxon.* Oxford, 1911.

TEXTS

1. KING ALFRED'S PREFACE TO GREGORY'S *PASTORAL*

Ælfred kyning hāteð grētan Wærferð biscep his wordum
luflīce ond frēondlīce ; ond ðē cȳðan hāte ðæt mē cōm swīðe
oft on gemynd, hwelce wiotan iū wæron giond Angelcynn,
ægðer ge godcundra hāda ge woruldcundra ; ond hū gesælig-
5 lica tīda ðā wæron giond Angelcynn ; ond hū ðā kyningas
ðe ðone onwald hæfdon ðæs folces on ðām dagum Gode ond
his ærendwrecum hȳrsumedon ; ond hū hīe ægðer ge hiora
sibbe ge hiora siodo ge hiora onweald innanbordes gehīoldon,
ond ēac ūt hiora ēðel gerȳmdon ; ond hū him ðā spēow
10 ægðer ge mid wīge ge mid wīsdōme ; ond ēac ðā godcundan
hādas hū giorne hīe wæron ægðer ge ymb lāre ge ymb liornunga,
ge ymb ealle ðā ðīowotdōmas ðe hīe Gode dōn scoldon ; ond
hū man ūtanbordes wīsdōm ond lāre hieder on lond sōhte,
ond hū wē hȳ nū sceoldon ūte begietan, gif wē hīe habban
15 sceoldon. Swæ clǣne hīo wæs oðfeallenu on Angelcynne ðæt
swīðe fēawe wæron behionan Humbre ðe hiora ðēninga cūðen
understondan on Englisc oððe furðum ān ǣrendgewrit of
Lǣdene on Englisc āreccean ; ond ic wēne ðæt nōht monige
begiondan Humbre nǣren. Swæ fēawe hiora wæron ðæt ic
20 furðum ānne ānlēpne ne mæg geðencean be sūðan Temese, ðā
ðā ic tō rīce fēng. Gode ælmihtegum sīe ðonc ðæt wē nū
ǣnigne onstāl habbað lārēowa. Ond for-ðon ic ðē bebīode
ðæt ðū dō swæ ic gelīefe ðæt ðū wille, ðæt ðū ðē ðissa woruld-
ðinga tō ðǣm geǣmetige, swæ ðū oftost mæge, ðæt ðū ðone
25 wīsdōm ðe ðē God sealde ðǣr ðǣr ðū hiene befæstan mæge,
befæste. Geðenc hwelce wītu ūs ðā becōmon for ðisse worulde,

7. hu *not in manuscript.*   16, 19. feawa.

ðā ðā wē hit nōhwæðer ne selfe ne lufodon, ne ēac ōðrum
monnum ne lēfdon ; ðone naman ānne wē lufodon ðæt wē
Crīstne wæren, ond swīðe fēawe ðā ðēawas.

30 Đā ic ðā ðis eall gemunde, ðā gemunde ic ēac hū ic
geseah, ær-ðæm-ðe hit eall forhergod wære ond forbærned,
hū ðā ciricean giond eall Angelcynn stōdon māðma ond
bōca gefylda, ond ēac micel menigeo Godes ðīowa ; ond
ðā swīðe lȳtle fiorme ðāra bōca wiston, for-ðæm-ðe hīe
35 hiora nānwuht ongiotan ne meahton, for-ðæm-ðe hȳ
næron on hiora āgen geðīode āwritene. Swelce hīe cwǣden :
' Ūre yldran, ðā ðe ðās stōwa ær hīoldon, hīe lufodon wīsdōm,
ond ðurh ðone hīe begēaton welan ond ūs lǣfdon. Hēr
mon mæg gīet gesīon hiora swæð, ac wē him ne cunnon æfter
40 spyrigean, ond for-ðæm wē habbað nū ǣgðer forlǣten ge
ðone welan ge ðone wīsdōm for-ðæm-ðe wē noldon tō ðǣm
spore mid ūre mōde onlūtan.'

Đā ic ðā ðis eall gemunde, ðā wundrade ic swīðe swīðe
ðāra gōdena wiotona ðe giū wæron giond Angelcynn, ond ðā
45 bēc ealla be fullan geliornod hæfdon, ðæt hīe hiora ðā nænne
dæl noldon on hiora āgen geðīode wendan. Ac ic ðā sōna eft
mē selfum andwyrde, ond cwæð : ' Hīe ne wēndon ðæt ǣfre
menn sceolden swǣ reccelēase weorðan ond sīo lār swǣ
oðfeallan ; for ðǣre wilnunga hȳ hit forlēton, ond woldon
50 ðæt hēr ðȳ māra wīsdōm on londe wǣre ðȳ wē mā geðēoda
cūðon.'

Đā gemunde ic hū sīo ǣ wæs ǣrest on Ēbrēisc geðīode
funden, ond eft, ðā hīe Greccas geliornodon, ðā wendon hīe
hīe on hiora āgen geðīode ealle, ond ēac ealle ōðre bēc.
55 Ond eft Lǣdenware swǣ same, siððan hīe hīe geliornodon, hīe
hīe wendon ealla ðurh wīse wealhstodas on hiora āgen geðīode.
Ond ēac ealla ōðra Crīstna ðīoda sumne dæl hiora on hiora
āgen geðīode wendon. For-ðȳ mē ðyncð betre, gif īow swǣ
ðyncð, ðæt wē ēac suma bēc, ðā ðe nīedbeðearfosta sīen eallum
60 monnum tō wiotonne, ðæt wē ðā on ðæt geðīode wenden ðe wē
ealle gecnāwan mægen, ond gedōn, swǣ wē swīðe ēaðe magon
mid Godes fultume, gif wē ðā stilnesse habbað, ðæt eall sīo
gioguð ðe nū is on Angelcynne frīora monna, ðāra ðe ðā spēda
hæbben ðæt hīe ðǣm befēolan mægen, sīen tō liornunga oðfæste,
65 ðā hwīle ðe hīe tō nānre ōðerre note ne mægen, oð ðone first

---

29. feawa.   33. gefyldæ.   45. eallæ.   47. ðætt.
48. re ce lease.   56. eall.   57. oðræ cristnæ.   59. sumæ.

ðe hīe wel cunnen Englisc gewrit ārǣdan. Lǣre mon siððan
furður on Lǣdengeðīode ðā ðe mon furðor lǣran wille ond tō
hīerran hāde dōn wille. Ðā ic ðā gemunde hū sīo lār Lǣdenge-
ðīodes ǣr ðissum āfeallen wæs giond Angelcyn, ond ðēah
70 monige cūðon Englisc gewrit ārǣdan, ðā ongan ic ongemang
ōðrum mislicum ond manigfealdum bisgum ðisses kynerīces ðā
bōc wendan on Englisc ðe is genemned on Lǣden *Pastoralis*,
ond on Englisc ' Hierdebōc,' hwīlum word be worde, hwīlum
andgit of andgiete, swǣ swǣ ic hīe geliornode æt Plegmunde
75 mīnum ærcebiscepe, ond æt Assere mīnum biscepe, ond æt
Grimbolde mīnum mæsseprīoste, ond æt Iōhanne mīnum mæsse-
prēoste. Siððan ic hīe ðā geliornod hæfde, swǣ swǣ ic hīe
forstōd, ond swǣ ic hīe andgitfullicost āreccean meahte,
ic hīe on Englisc āwende ; ond tō ǣlcum biscepstōle on
80 mīnum rīce wille āne onsendan ; ond on ǣlcre bið ān æstel,
sē bið on fīftegum mancessa. Ond ic bebīode on Godes naman
ðæt nān mon ðone æstel from ðǣre bēc ne dō, ne ðā bōc from
ðǣm mynstre ; uncūð hū longe ðǣr swǣ gelǣrede biscepas
sīen, swǣ swǣ nū, Gode ðonc, welhwǣr siendon. For-ðȳ ic
85 wolde ðæt hīe ealneg æt ðǣre stōwe wǣren, būton sē biscep
hīe mid him habban wille, oððe hīo hwǣr tō lǣne sīe, oððe
hwā ōðre bī wrīte.

2. A DESCRIPTION OF BRITAIN

Breoton is gārsecges ēalond, ðæt wæs iūgeāra Albion
hāten : is geseted betwyh norðdǣle and westdǣle, Germānie
and Gallie and Hispānie, þām mǣstum dǣlum Eurōpe, myccle
fǣce ongegen. Þæt is norð ehta hund mīla lang, and tū hund
5 mīla brād. Hit hafað fram sūðdǣle þā mǣgðe ongēan þe
mon hāteð Gallia Belgica. Hit is welig, þis ēalond, on
wæstmum and on trēowum misenlicra cynna, and hit is
gescrǣpe on lǣswe scēapa and nēata, and on sumum stōwum
wīngeardas grōwað. Swylce ēac þēos eorðe is berende missen-
10 licra fugela and sǣwihta, and fiscwyllum wæterum and wyllge-
spryngum ; and hēr bēoð oft fangene seolas and hronas and

---

68. hieran.   81. mancessan.   6. Bellica.   8. gescræwe.

mereswȳn, and hēr bēoð oft numene missenlicra cynna
weolcscylle and muscule, and on þām bēoð oft gemētte þā
betstan meregrotan ælces hīwes. And hēr bēoð swȳðe
15 genihtsume weolocas, of þām bið geworht sē weoloc-rēada
tælhg, þone ne mæg sunne blæcan ne ne regen wyrdan ; ac
swā hē bið yldra, swā hē fægerra bið. Hit hafað ēac, þis land,
sealtsēaðas, and hit hafað hāt wæter, and hāt baðo, ælcere
yldo and hāde þurh tōdælede stōwe gescræpe. Swylce hit is
20 ēac berende on wecga ōrum, āres and īsernes, lēades and
seolfres. Hēr bið ēac gemēted gagates ; sē stān bið blæc
gym. Gif mon hine on fȳr dēð, þonne flēoð þær neddran
onweg.

Wæs þis ēalond ēac gēo gewurðad mid þām æðelestum
25 ceastrum, ānes wana þrittigum, ðā þe wæron mid weallum and
torrum and geatum and þām trumestum locum getimbrade,
būtan ōðrum læssan unrīm ceastrum. And for-ðan-þe ðis
ēalond under þām sylfum norðdæle middangeardes nȳhst
ligeð, lēohte nihte on sumera hafað, swā þæt oft on middre
30 nihte geflit cymeð þām behealdendum, hwæðer hit sī þe æfen-
glōmung ðe on morgen deagung : is on ðon sweotol ðæt þis
ēalond hafað mycele lengran dagas on sumera, and swā ēac
nihta on wintra, þonne þā sūðdælas middangeardes.

3. FROM THE NEW TESTAMENT

A. THE LORD'S PRAYER

The Gospel of St. Matthew, vi. 9-13

Fæder ūre þū þe eart on heofonum sī þīn nama gehālgod.
Tōbecume þīn rīce. Gewurþe ðīn willa on eorðan swā swā on
heofonum. Urne gedæghwāmlican hlāf syle ūs tō-dæg. And
forgyf ūs ūre gyltas, swā swā wē forgyfað ūrum gyltendum.
5 And ne gelæd þū ūs on costnunge, ac ālȳs ūs of yfele. Sōþlīce.

---

16. regen *not in manuscript.*
29. and leohte.
27. ceastra.
31. æfen glommung.

B. THE PRODIGAL SON

The Gospel of St. Luke, xv. 11-38

Sōðlīce sum man hæfde twēgen suna. Þā cwæð sē gingra
tō his fæder ; ' Fæder, syle mē mīnne dǣl mīnre ǣhte þe mē tō
gebyreð '. Þā dǣlde hē him his ǣhte. Ðā æfter fēawum
dagum ealle his þing gegaderude sē gingra sunu, and fērde
10 wrǣclīce on feorlen rīce, and forspilde þār his ǣhta, lybbende on
his gǣlsan. Ðā hē hig hæfde ealle āmyrrede, þā wearð mycel
hunger on þām rīce, and hē wearð wǣdla. Þā fērde hē and
folgude ānum burhsittendan men þæs rīces ; ðā sende hē hine
tō his tūne þæt hē hēolde his swȳn. Ðā gewilnode hē his
15 wambe gefyllan of þām bīen-coddum þe ðā swȳn ǣton ; and
him man ne sealde. Þā beþōhte hē hine, and cwæð, ' Ēalā, hū
fela yrðlinga on mīnes fæder hūse hlāf genōhne habbað ; and
ic hēr on hungre forwurðe ! Ic ārīse, and ic fare tō mīnum fæder
and ic secge him : " Ēalā, fæder, ic syngode on heofenas and
20 beforan þē ; nū ic neom wyrðe þæt ic bēo þīn sunu nemned ;
dō mē swā ānne of þīnum yrðlingum." ' And hē ārās þā, and
cōm tō his fæder. And þā gȳt þā hē wæs feorr his fæder, hē
hyne geseah, and wearð mid mildheortnesse āstyrod, and agen
hine arn, and hine beclypte, and cyste hine. Ðā cwæð his
25 sunu : ' Fæder, ic syngude on heofen and beforan ðē ; nū ic ne
eom wyrþe þæt ic þīn sunu bēo genemned '. Ðā cwæð sē fæder
tō his þēowum : ' Bringað raðe þǣne sēlestan gegyrelan and
scrȳdað hyne, and syllað him hring on his hand and gescȳ tō
his fōtum ; and bringað ān fǣtt styric and ofslēað, and utun
30 etan and gewistfullian ; for-þām þes mīn sunu wæs dēad, and
hē geedcucude ; hē forwearð, and hē is gemēt '. Ðā ongunnon
hig gewistlǣcan. Sōðlīce hys yldra sunu wæs on æcere ; and
hē cōm, and þā hē þām hūse genēalǣhte, hē gehȳrde þǣne swēg
and þæt weryd. Þā clypode hē ānne þēow, and āxode hine hwæt
35 þæt wǣre. Ðā cwæð hē : ' Þīn brōðor cōm ; and þīn fæder
ofslōh ān fǣt celf, for-þām-þe hē hyne hālne onfēng '. Ðā
gebealh hē hine, and nolde in gān. Þā ēode his fæder ūt, and
ongan hine biddan. Ðā cwæþ hē his fæder andswarigende :
' Efne swā fela gēara ic þē þēowude, and ic nǣfre þīn bebod
40 ne forgȳmde ; and ne sealdest þū mē nǣfre ān ticcen þæt ic mid

6. yldra.   8. feawa.   15. bien coddun.

mīnum frēondum gewistfullude ; ac syððan þes þīn sunu cōm,
þe hys spēde mid myltystrum āmyrde, þū ofslōge him fǣtt
celf '. Ðā cwæþ hē : ' Sunu, þū eart symle mid mē, and ealle
mīne þing synd þīne ; þē gebyrede gewistfullian and geblissian,
45 for-þām þes þīn brōðor wæs dēad, and hē geedcucede ; hē
forwearð, and hē is gemēt '.

4. FROM APOLLONIUS OF TYRE

Mid-þī-ðe sē cyning þās word gecwæð, ðā fǣringa þār
ēode in ðæs cynges iunge dohtor and cyste hyre fæder
and ðā ymbsittendan. Þā hēo becōm tō Apollonio, þā
gewǣnde hēo ongēan tō hire fæder and cwæð : ' Ðū gōda
5 cyninge and mīn sē lēofesta fæder, hwæt is þes iunga man
þe ongēan ðē on swā wurðlicum setle sit mid sārlīcum and-
wlitan ? Nāt ic hwæt hē besorgað.' Ða cwæð sē cyninge :
' Lēofe dohtor, þes iunga man is forliden, and hē gecwēmde
mē manna betst on ðām plegan, for-ðām ic hine gelaðode
10 tō ðysum ūrum gebēorscipe. Nāt ic hwæt hē is ne hwanon
hē is ; ac gif ðū wille witan hwæt hē sȳ, āxsa hine, for-ðām
þē gedafenað þæt þū wite.' Ðā ēode þæt mǣden tō Apollonio
and mid forwandigendre sprǣce cwæð : ' Ðēah ðū stille
sȳ and unrōt, þēah ic þīne æðelborennesse on ðē gesēo.
15 Nū þonne, gif ðē tō hefig ne þince, sege mē þīnne naman, and
þīn gelymp ārece mē.' Ða cwæð Apollonius : ' Gif ðū for
nēode āxsast æfter mīnum namon, ic secge þē ic hine forlēas
on sǣ. Gif ðū wilt mīne æðelborennesse witan, wite ðū
þæt ic hig forlēt on Tharsum.' Ðæt mǣden cwæð : ' Sege
20 me gewislīcor, þæt ic hit mæge understandan.' Apollonius
þā sōðlīce hyre ārehte ealle his gelymp, and æt þāre sprǣce
ende him fēollon tēaras of ðām ēagum. Mid-þȳ-þe sē cynge
þæt geseah, hē bewǣnde hine ðā tō ðāre dehter and cwæð :
' Lēofe dohtor, þū gesingodest mid-þȳ-þe þū woldest witan
25 his naman and his gelimp ; þū hafast nū geednīwod his
ealde sār. Ac ic bidde þē þæt þū gife him swā-hwæt-swā ðū
wille.' Ðā ðā þæt mǣden gehīrde þæt hire wæs ālȳfed fram
hire fæder þæt hēo ǣr hyre silf gedōn wolde, ðā cwæð hēo tō

8, 24. leofa.   13. stilli.   21. sprǣcan.   23. dohtor.

Apollonio : 'Apolloni, sōðlīce þū eart ūre ; forlǣt þīne
30 murcnunge ; and, nū ic mīnes fæder lēafe habbe, ic gedō
ðē weligne.'
   Apollonius hire þæs þancode ; and sē cynge blissode on
his dohtor welwillendnesse, and hyre tō cwæð : 'Lēofe
dohtor, hāt feccan þīne hearpan, and gecīg ðē tō þīne frȳnd,
35 and āfirsa fram þām iungan his sārnesse.' Ðā ēode hēo ūt
and hēt feccan hire hearpan ; and sōna swā hēo hearpian
ongan, hēo mid winsumum sange gemǣngde þāre hearpan
swēg. Ðā ongunnon ealle þā men hī herian on hyre swēgcræft, and Apollonius āna swīgode. Ðā cwæð sē cyninge :
40 'Apolloni, nū ðū dēst yfele, for-ðām-þe ealle men heriað mīne
dohtor on hyre swēgcræfte, and þū āna hī swīgende tǣlst.'
Apollonius cwæð : 'Ēalā ! ðū gōda cynge, gif ðū mē gelīfst,
ic secge þæt ic ongite þæt sōðlīce þīn dohtor gefēol on swēgcræft, ac hēo næfð hine nā wel geleornod. Ac hāt mē nū
45 sillan þā hearpan ; þonne wāst þū nū þæt þū gīt nāst.'
Arcestrates sē cyning cwæð : 'Apolloni, ic oncnāwe sōðlīce
þæt þū eart on eallum þingum wel gelǣred '. Ðā hēt sē
cyng sillan Apollonige þā hearpan. Apollonius þā ūt ēode,
and hine scrīdde and sette ǣnne cynehelm uppon his hēafod
50 and nam þā hearpan on his hand, and in ēode, and swā stōd
þæt sē cynge and ealle þā ymbsittendan wēndon þæt hē
nǣre Apollonius, ac þæt hē wǣre Apollines, ðāra hǣðenra
god. Ðā wearð stilnes and swīge geworden innon ðāre
healle ; and Apollonius his hearpenægl genam, and hē þā
55 hearpestrengas mid cræfte āstirian ongan and þāre hearpan
swēg mid winsumum sange gemǣngde. And sē cynge silf
and ealle þe þār andwearde wǣron micelre stæfne cliopodon
and hine heredon. Æfter þisum forlēt Apollonius þā hearpan,
and plegode, and fela fægera þinga þār forð tēah, þe þām
60 folce ungecnāwen wæs and ungewunelic ; and heom eallum
þearle līcode ǣlc þāra þinga ðe hē forð tēah.
   Sōðlīce, mid-þȳ-þe þæs cynges dohtor geseah þæt
Apollonius on eallum gōdum cræftum swā wel wæs getogen, þā
gefēol hyre mōd on his lufe. Ðā æfter þæs bēorscipes geen-
65 dunge cwæð þæt mǣden tō ðām cynge : 'Lēofa fæder,

---

33. leofa.   34. þinum frynd.   36. heapian.
37. gemægnde.   56. gemægnde.
59. plegod *followed by an erasure of about fifteen letters.*
60. ungecnawe.

þū lȳfdest mē lītle ǣr þæt ic mōste gifan Apollonio swā-hwæt-
swā ic wolde óf þīnum goldhorde '. Arcestrates sē cyng
cwæð tō hyre : ' Gif him swā-hwæt-swā ðū wille '. Hēo ðā
swīðe blīðe ūt ēode and cwæð : ' Lārēow Apolloni, ic gife þē
70 be mīnes fæder lēafe twā hund punda goldes and fēower
hund punda gewihte seolfres, and þone mǣstan dǣl dēorwurðan rēafes, and twentig ðēowa manna '. And hēo þā
þus cwæð tō ðām þēowum mannum : ' Beráð þās þingc mid
ēow, þe ic behēt Apollonio mīnum lārēowe, and lecgað innon
75 būre beforan mīnum frēondum '. Þis wearð þā þus gedōn
æfter þāre cwēne hǣse, and ealle þā men hire gife heredon ðe
hig gesāwon. Ðā sōðlīce geendode sē gebēorscipe ; and þā
men ealle ārison, and grētton þone cyngc and ðā cwēne and
bǣdon hig gesunde bēon, and hām gewǣndon. Eac swilce
80 Apollonius cwæð : ' Ðū gōda cyngc and earmra gemiltsigend,
and þū cwēn lāre lufigend, bēon gē gesunde '. Hē beseah ēac
tō ðām þēowum mannum, þe þæt mǣden him forgifen hæfde,
and heom cwæð tō : ' Nimað þās þing mid ēow, þe mē sēo
cwēn forgeaf, and gān wē sēcan ūre gesthūs þæt wē magon ūs
85 gerestan '.

5. FROM ÆLFRIC'S COLLOQUY

Discipulus. Wē cildra biddaþ þē, ēalā lārēow, þæt þū
tǣce ūs sprecan rihte, for-þām ungelǣrede wē syndon and
gewæmmodlīce wē sprecaþ.
Magister. Hwæt wille gē sprecan ?
5 *D.* Hwæt rēce wē hwæt wē sprecan, būton hit riht sprǣc
sȳ and behēfe, næs īdel oþþe fracod ?
M. Wille gē bēon beswungen on leornunge ?
   D. Lēofre ys ūs bēon beswungen for lāre þænne hit
ne cunnan ; ac wē witan þē bilewitne wesan, and nellan
10 onbelǣdan swincgla ūs, būton þū bī tōgenȳdd fram ūs.
   M. Ic āxie þē, hwæt sprycst þū ? Hwæt hæfst þū
weorkes ?

---

69. sweoðe.   77. þe gebeorscipe.   2. rihte *not in manuscript.*
 6. behese.   7. gē beon *not in manuscript.*
 8. beswugen.   10. onbelǣden.

D. Ic eom geanwyrde munuc, and ic sincge ǣlce dæg
seofon tīda mid gebrōþrum, and ic eom bysgod on rǣdinge
15 and on sange ; ac þeahhwæþere ic wolde betwēnan leornian
sprecan on Ledengereorde.

M. Hwæt cunnon þās þīne gefēran ?

D. Sume synt yrþlincgas, sume scēphyrdas, sume ox-
anhyrdas, sume ēac swylce huntan, sume fisceras, sume
20 fugeleras, sume cȳpmenn, sume sceōwyrhtan, sealteras,
bæceras.

M. Hwæt sægest þū, yrþlincg ? Hū begæst þū weorc þīn ?

D. Ealā lēof hlāford, þearle ic deorfe. Ic gā ūt on
dægræd þȳwende oxon tō felda, and iucie hig tō syl. Nys
25 hit swā stearc winter þæt ic durre lūtian æt hām for ege
hlāfordes mīnes ; ac, geiukodan oxan and gefæstnodon
sceare and cultre mid þǣre syl, ǣlce dæg ic sceal erian fulne
æcer oþþe māre.

M. Hæfst þū ǣnigne gefēran ?

30 *D.* Ic hæbbe sumne cnapan þȳwende oxan mid gādīsene,
þe ēac swilce nū hās ys for cylde and hrēame.

M. Hwæt māre dēst þū on dæg ?

D. Gewyslīce þænne māre ic dō. Ic sceal fyllan binnan
oxan mid hīg, and wæterian hig, and scearn heora beran ūt.

35 *M.* Hig ! Hig ! Micel gedeorf ys hyt.

D. Gēa, lēof, micel gedeorf hit ys for-þām ic neom
frēoh. . . .

M. Hwylcne cræft canst þū ?

D. Ic eom fiscere.

40 *M.* Hwæt begyst þū of þīnum cræfte ?

D. Bigleofan and scrūd and feoh.

M. Hū gefēhst þū fixas ?

D. Ic āstīgie mīn scyp, and wyrpe max mīne on ēa, and
ancgil ic wyrpe and spyrtan, and swā-hwæt-swā hig gehæfta\ð
45 ic genime.

M. Hwæt gif hit unclǣne bēoþ fixas ?

D. Ic ūtwyrpe þā unclǣnan ūt and genime mē clǣne
tō mete.

---

13. monuc.	14. on rædinge *not in manuscript.*	
20. scewyrhtan.	24. iugie.	27. mit.
28. æþer.	34. wæte terian, sceasn.	36. Ge.
44. ancgil *vel* æs.	46. heoþ.	47. ut clǣnan.

M. Hwǣr cȳpst þū fixas þīne ?

50 *D.* On ceastre.

M. Hwā bigþ hī ?

D. Ceasterwara. Ic ne mæg swā fela gefōn swā ic mæg gesyllan.

M. Hwilce fixas gefēhst þū ?

55 *D.* Ǣlas and hacodas, mynas and ǣlepūtan, scēotan and lampredan, and swā-wylce-swā on wætere swymmaþ sprote.

M. For hwī ne fixast þū on sǣ?

D. Hwīlon ic dō, ac seldon, for-þām micel rēwyt mē ys tō sǣ.

60 *M.* Hwæt fēhst þū on sǣ?

D. Hæringcas and leaxas, mereswȳn and stirian, ostran and crabban, muslan, winewinclan, sǣcoccas, fagc and flōc and lopystran, and fela swylces. . . .

M. Þū, cnapa, hwæt dydest tō-dæg ?

65 *D.* Manega þing ic dyde. On þisse niht, þā þā cnyll ic gehȳrde, ic ārās of mīnon bedde and ēode tō cyrcean, and sang ūhtsang mid gebrōþrum ; æfter þā wē sungon be eallum hālgum and dægredlice lofsangas ; æfter ðȳsum prīm and seofon seolmas mid lētanīan, and capitolmæssan; syþþan 70 undertīde, and dydon mæssan be dæge ; æfter þisum wē sungan middæg, and ǣton and druncon and slēpon, and eft wē ārison and sungon nōn ; and nū wē synd hēr ætforan þē gearuwe gehȳran hwæt þū ūs secge.

M. Hwænne wylle gē syngan æfen- oþþe niht-sangc ?

75 *D.* Þonne hyt tīma byþ.

M. Wǣre þū tō-dæg beswuncgen?

D. Ic næs, for-þām wærlīce ic mē hēold.

M. And hū þīne gefēran?

D. Hwæt mē āhsast be þām? Ic ne dear yppan þē 80 dīgla ūre. Anra gehwylc wāt gif hē beswuncgen wæs oþþe nā.

M. Hwæt ytst þū on dæg?

D. Gȳt flǣscmettum ic brūce, for-ðām cild ic eom under gyrda drohtniende.

M. Hwæt māre ytst þū!

---

52. swa fela swa ic mæg swa fela swa ic mæg gesyllan.
64. dydest dæg.   66. aras on, cycean.   68 lofsanges.
70. mæssa.   71. drucon.   79. deor.

85   **D.** Wyrta and ǣigra, fisc and cȳse, buteran and bēana
and ealle clǣne þingc ic ete mid micelre þancunge.

M. Swȳþe waxgeorn eart þū, þonne þū ealle þingc etst
þe þē tōforan gesette synd.

87. paxgeorn.   88. gesette synd *not in manuscript.*

1. KING ALFRED'S PREFACE TO GREGORY'S *PASTORAL*

King Alfred's English version of the *Regulae Pastoralis Liber* of Gregory the Great is the only early West Saxon work that is preserved in two manuscripts contemporary with the author, Bodleian Hatton 20 and B.M. Cotton Tiberius B.XI. The text of both manuscripts is given by Henry Sweet in his edition for the Early English Text Society (1871-2). Our text is based on the Hatton MS., and the opening of the Preface is reproduced as a frontispiece. This Preface has very great historical interest. It is one of the few examples that we possess of King Alfred's original compositions, as distinct from translations, and it throws light on his character. He is zealous for reform but anxious not to impose too great a burden on his people ; the education that he introduces is by no means to be universal (ll. 62-66). A similar moderation is to be seen at the end of the Preface (ll. 81-87). After saying that the book must not be removed from the church he goes on to mention a number of exceptions to this prohibition. King Alfred's prose is forthright and headlong, with little stylistic artifice. The translations may well have been dictated, and the style is that of the spoken rather than the written language.

At the head of the Preface in the Hatton MS. occur the words *Ðēos bōc sceal tō Wiogoraceastre:* 'This book is intended for Worcester.' This heading is explained by l. 79 of the text ; MS. Hatton 20 was the manuscript intended for Wærferð, Bishop of Worcester. Since it is written in a hand of King Alfred's time, it is a very valuable source of information about early West Saxon, free from the influence of later scribes, who often modified the spelling of the manuscripts they copied.

1 f. Ælfred kyning . . . hāte. This is the conventional opening of an Old English formal letter. The transition to the first person (*hāte*, l. 2) after the formal opening is also conventional.

1. The object of *hāteð* is to be understood ; cf. 4. 44 and § 238.

Wærferð, Bishop of Worcester, translated into Old English the *Dialogues* of Gregory the Great.

2. cōm. The subject is the noun clause *hwelce . . .*
Angelcynn.

3. wiotan. Nom. pl. of *wita* ' scholar '. The *io* is due to
back mutation (§ 45) ; cf. *siodo* 1. 8.

iū. A variant spelling of *geō* ' formerly ' (§ 83(*b*)).

giond. The use of *io, īo* for *eo, ēo* is fairly common in
early WS. and is a feature of the spelling of this manuscript ;
cf. *gehīoldon* 1. 8.

6. onwald. An Anglian form (§ 33) ; the normal WS.
form is *onweald*, which occurs at 1. 8, with fronting and
fracture. Even in early WS. texts some Anglian forms are
to be found (§ 6).

7. hȳrsumedon. On the *e* see § 196 Note.

9. him . . . spēow. An impersonal construction (§ 239) :
' there was success to them ', i.e. ' they succeeded '.

11. liornunga. On the ending *-a* see § 109 Note 5 and cf.
wilnunga 1. 49.

13. hieder on lond ' here in this land '.

14. On the variation between **hīe** and **hȳ** see § 51 and § 136
Note 4. **hȳ** and **hīe** could be acc. pl. referring to *wīsdōm ond*
lāre, but in view of the sing. *hīo wæs* in the next sentence, they
are probably acc. sing. feminine, referring to *lāre*.

oðfeallenu nom. sing. feminine. The past participle is
declined like an adjective (§ 123).

19. nǣren. The subjunctive is used after a verb of thinking (§ 235(*c*)).

20 f. ðā ðā ' when '. Similarly *ðǣr ðǣr* 1. 25 means
' where ' (§ 220).

21. sīe 3 sing. pres. subj. of the verb ' to be '. It is here
used jussively (§ 234).

24 ff. ðæt ðū in 1. 24 is parallel with the first *ðæt ðū* in
1. 23 and both begin noun clauses which are dependent on
bebīode 1. 22. The words *swæ ðū oftost mæge* are a parenthesis,
and *tō ðǣm* 1. 24 is correlative with *ðæt* in the same line ;
tō ðǣm ðæt means ' in order that '. The whole sentence
beginning on 1. 22 may be translated : ' And accordingly I
command you to do as I believe that you will, (namely) to
free yourself from these worldly affairs, as often as you can,
in order that you may apply the wisdom which God gave you
where you can apply it.'

25. hiene. OE. had grammatical gender, and the acc.
sing. masculine pronoun *hiene* refers to the masculine noun

wīsdōm 1. 25.   The beginnings of natural gender, as we know it today, are to be seen in the use of *hit* in 1. 27 to refer to the masculine noun *wīsdōm*.

27. **nōhwæðer . . . ne** 'neither . . . nor '.   On the repetition of *ne* see § 222.

selfe agrees with the subject *wē* (§ 230).

29. **swīðe fēawe ðā ðēawas** 'very few (of us loved) the virtues '.

31. **hit eall** refers to *Angelcynn* (neuter) in the next line.

33. **gefylda** ' filled ', nom. pl. of the pp. *gefylled* with syncope of lightly stressed *e* (§ 72) and simplification of *ll* (§ 101).

menigeo is nom. ; the verb *wæs* is to be understood.

34. **ðā** ' they ' (§ 230).

40. **for-ðǣm** ' for that reason ' is to be distinguished from *for-ðǣm-ðe* ' because ' 1. 35.

43. **wundrade.**   Forms with *a* are especially common in non-WS. (§ 196 Note).

49. **for ðǣre wilnunga** ' because of the desire (*sc.* that learning should not decline) '.

50. **ðȳ . . . ðȳ** are correlative and have the same function as MnE. *the . . . the* with comparatives.

māra is a comp. adj. meaning ' greater ' ; *mā* is a comp. adv. which, when followed by a noun in the genitive, means ' more '.

53 f. **ðā wendon hīe hīe.**   The first *hīe* is nom. pl. referring to *Greccas;* the second *hīe* is acc. sing. feminine referring to *ǣ*.

55 f. **hīe hīe wendon.**   The second *hīe* is acc. pl. referring to *bēc*, which here means ' books of the Bible ' ; in 1. 59 *bēc* means ' books ' in general.

58. **īow.**   Alfred is now addressing all the bishops ; in 1. 2 he was addressing only one of them.

60. **ðæt wē ðā** repeats the sense of *ðæt wē suma bēc* of 1. 59 lest the intervening relative clause should obscure the sense.

65. **ne mægen** sc. *oðfæste wesan*.

first is a noun ' time '.

73 f. **hwilum . . . andgiete** sometimes closely and sometimes freely.

74-76.   It is interesting to note that Alfred's helpers named here all came from outside the boundaries of Wessex. Plegmund, Archbishop of Canterbury from 890 until his death in 914,

was a Mercian.   Asser (d. 909 or 910) was a Welsh priest who
agreed to spend six months of each year in Alfred's household
and six months in his own country ; he was the author of a
Latin biography of Alfred into which many legends about
the king were later incorporated.   Grimbold or Grimbald
(d. 903) was a monk of the Flemish monastery of St. Bertin
who came over to England about 893 and became Abbot of New
Minster at Winchester.   John was an Old Saxon who was made
Abbot of the monastery which Alfred founded at Athelney.

80. **biŏ** ' there will be '.   The present tense is used to
express the future (§ 232).

æstel.   This word is probably derived from late Latin
astella, ' chip, plank, board ', or from Latin *hastula* ' little
spear ', and it survives as *astel* in ME. and MnE. dialects
in the sense ' board, plank '.   The only other occurrence in
OE. is in Ælfric's *Glossary*, where it is used to translate
Latin *indicatorium*, a word otherwise unknown.   Of the many
suggested meanings of the OE. word, two deserve considera-
tion : (*a*) the front board of a book-cover and (*b*) book-mark.
The first of these suggestions fits in better with the high value
of the *œstel;* the second fits in better with Ælfric's *indicatorium*
in so far as the meaning of this word can be deduced from related Latin words.

81. **on** ' of the value of '.

mancessa gen. pl. of *mancus*, a gold coin of foreign origin
equivalent to thirty silver pence.   It is used in OE. as money
of account, and in the tenth century it is quoted as the value of
an ox.   The word is interesting as the earliest example of an
Arabic loan-word in English ; it is derived from an Arabic
word meaning ' stamped (with a die) '.

85. **hīe** is shown by the verb *wæren* to be pl., probably
referring to the book and the *œstel; hīe* 1. 86 may be either
acc. sing. or pl. ; *hīo* 1. 86 must be sing., as shown by the
verb *sīe*, and refers to the book alone.

2. A DESCRIPTION OF BRITAIN

This passage is the opening of the Old English translation
of Bede's *Historia Ecclesiastica*, which was completed in 731 ;
the Old English translation was made in the reign of Alfred

and probably under his direction. It is preserved in four manuscripts, the earliest of which is at least a century later than the date of the translation. Readings from all four manuscripts are given by J. Schipper in Grein's *Prosa* (Leipzig, 1897) ; the edition by T. Miller (Early English Text Society, 1890-8) is based mainly on Bodleian MS. Tanner 10. Our text is based on MS. Cambridge Univ. Lib. Kk. 3. 18.

3 f. **myccle fæce.** Instrumental of measure of difference : ' some distance away '. The prep. *ongegen* governs the preceding noun *d$\bar{æ}$lum* (§ 231). The *cc* is due to the influence of the following *l* (§ 104).

4. **ehta,** earlier *eahta.* The *ea* has become *e* before *h* by a late WS. change (§ 53).

hund accusative of extent (§ 224) ; **mīla** is partitive gen. (§ 133).

6. **Gallia Belgica.** One of the three divisions of Gaul, which Caesar (*De Bello Gallico*, Book I) described as inhabited by the Belgae.

9. **berende** ' productive of '.

10. The words ' it is famous for ' are to be understood before *fiscwyllum.* The Latin has *fluviis quoque multum piscosis ac fontibus praeclara copiosis.*

14. **meregrota.** The word is borrowed from Latin *margarita,* which is derived from Greek, but the form of the OE. word has been modified by popular etymology, which has associated it with *mere* ' sea ' and *grot* ' particle '.

16. **tælhg.** The usual form is *telg;* on the *æ* see § 40. The *hg* is probably a spelling to indicate that the consonant is a fricative.

22. **neddran.** The earliest forms of the nom. sing. are *n$\bar{æ}$dre,* less often *n$\bar{e}$dre* (§ 30). The *r* caused doubling of the preceding consonant (§ 104) and the preceding vowel was then shortened (§ 65(*a*)).

25. **ānes wana þrittigum,** ' thirty less one ' ; *wana* is a sb. meaning ' want, deficiency ', which is here treated as an indeclinable adjective.

27. **læssan** dat. pl., earlier *l$\bar{æ}$ssum* (§ 122 Note 2).

unrim, ' a countless number ', is occasionally left undeclined, as here.

29. **nihte.** Since *niht* belongs to the monosyllabic consonant declension (§ 113), the acc. pl. would normally be *niht.*

The -*e* here and the -*a* in l. 33 are due to the analogy of the ō-declension (§ 109).

30 f. **þe . . . ðe** are correlative ; only the **second** *ðe* need be translated.

3. FROM THE NEW TESTAMENT

The West Saxon version of the Gospels is preserved in seven manuscripts, some of them incomplete. Our text is based on MS. Corpus Christi College Cambridge 140, a manuscript written at the beginning of the eleventh century, which forms the basis of the edition of J. W. Bright (4 vols., Boston, 1904-6). Another edition is that of W. W. Skeat (4 vols., Cambridge, 1871-1878).

A reader of the Old English translation of the Gospels will inevitably find himself comparing the rendering with that of the Authorized Version of 1611. Since this is acknowledged to be a masterpiece of English prose, it is natural that the Old English version should suffer by such a stylistic comparison, but the West Saxon Gospels are notable as showing that even at this early date, English prose was capable of rendering with clarity and simplicity the ideas expressed in the Vulgate.

1 f. **sī, tōbecume,** and **gewurþe** are 3 sing. pres. subj. used jussively (§ 234).

3. **syle.** The *y* is from earlier *e* (§ 195 Note 2).

7. **tō** governs the preceding word *mē* (§ 231).

9. **gegaderude.** An early form of *gegaderode* (§ 196 Note).

10. **lybbende** is an example of the use of *y* as a spelling for *i*, vey common in late WS. (§ 10).

11. **hig** is an inverted spelling for **hī** (§ 10).

13. **men** dat. sing. (§ 113).

14. **hēolde.** The subjunctive is used to express purpose (§ 235(*e*)).

17. **fæder** gen. sing. (§ 115).

18. **ārīse, fare** present for future (§ 232).

27. **þæne.** A late OE. variant of the acc. sing. masculine *þone* (§ 138 Note 2).

28. **hring.** The indefinite article is often omitted in OE. (§ 229).

29. **ān fǣtt styric** is the object of both *bringað* and *ofslēað*. On the *i* of *styric* see § 75.

utun, earlier *wutun,* with loss of *w* before *u* (§ 93). In origin *(w)utun, (w)uton* is the 1 pers. pl. optative of the verb *wītan,* ' to go ', and is frequently used in OE. with the sense ' let us '.

4. FROM APOLLONIUS OF TYRE

The Old English version of the romance *Apollonius of Tyre* is found only in MS. Corpus Christi College Cambridge 201 and was edited by Zupitza in Herrig's *Archiv,* vol. 97, p. 17. The story is thought to have been derived from a lost Greek original through a Latin version, which has been preserved in more than a hundred manuscripts. Although these manuscripts differ greatly from each other, the Latin text is often a useful aid to the elucidation of the Old English. The popularity of the romance is shown by the large number of Latin manuscript versions and by the recurrence of the story in many medieval and later works, including the *Gesta Romanorum* (cap. 153), Gower's *Confessio Amantis* (Book VIII), and the Shakespearean play *Pericles.*

The Old English version, which belongs to the first half of the eleventh century, is only a fragment, but it is of interest as a unique example of Old English romantic fiction. Our extract begins with a feast at the palace of Arcestrates, king of Tarsus. The king has just welcomed Apollonius, who has been shipwrecked on the shores of his kingdom.

4. gewænde. On the *æ* see § 40.

6. sit. Syncopated form of the 3 sing. pres. ind. of *sittan.* The 3 sing. was earlier *siteþ.* There was syncope of the unaccented *e* on the analogy of verbs with long stems (§ 72), followed by assimilation of *tþ* to *tt* (§ 90) and simplification of *tt* to *t* (§ 102).

11. āxsa. This form is the result of confusion between the variant spellings *ācsa* and *āxa,* where *x* is a spelling for *cs;* cf. *āxsast* 1. 17.

13 f. Đēah . . . þēah are correlative : ' although . . . yet'.

16. þīn gelymp neut. pl. ' your adventures (or misfortunes) '. The Latin has *casus tuos.*

17. namon. Dat. sing. of *nama.* On the *-on* see § 112 Note 4.

21. ealle. On the final *-e* see § 118 Note 2.

29. **þū eart ūre** ' you are (one) of us '.

32. **þancian** takes the dat. of the person and the gen. of the thing.

34. **hāt feccan.** See note on l. 44.

gecīg ðē tō þīne frȳnd ' call your friends to you ' (§ 231).

43. **gefēol** ' has chanced '. The Latin has *incidit*.

44. The object of *hāt* is to be understood : ' command the harp to be given to me ' ; cf. l. 1 and § 238.

45. **sillan.** On the *i* see § 195 Note 2.

wāst ' you will know ' (§ 232) ; *nū* goes with *n ī st*.

52. **Apollines** Apollo.

54. **hearpenægl** literally ' harp-nail '. This word illustrates the unwillingness of Old English authors to use loanwords. The Latin has *plectrum*, which is the word that we should use in Modern English.

59. **plegode** ' acted '.

60. **heom.** On the *eo* see § 136 Note 3.

70. **fæder** gen. sing. as in 3. 17 (§ 115).

71f. **dēorwurðan,** the weak form of the adjective, is used where we should expect the strong. This use is common in poetry but rare in prose (§ 227 (*e*)).

76. **æfter þāre cwēne hǣse** ' according to the command of the princess '. On the construction see § 229.

80. **gōda.** The weak form of the adj. is used in the vocative (§ 227(*d*)).

81. **bēon** 2 pl. pres. subj. When the subjunctive is used to express a wish it is usually in the third person (§ 234), but occasionally, as here, in the second person or, as in *gān* l. 84, in the first person.

82. **mǣden** from *mægden* ' maiden ' (§ 99).

83. **heom cwæð tō** ' said to them ' (§ 231).

5. FROM ÆLFRIC'S COLLOQUY

Ælfric's *Colloquy* is a Latin dialogue between a schoolmaster and his pupils preserved in four manuscripts. The only manuscript with a continuous interlinear gloss in Old English is B.M. Cotton Tiberius A.III, on which our text is based. Only the Old English text of part of the *Colloquy* is given here ; the complete Latin and Old English texts of the

Cotton manuscript have been edited by G. N. Garmonsway (Methuen's Old English Library, 1939). It is probable that the Latin *Colloquy* was the work of Ælfric, but that the English glosses, which in places reveal ignorance of Latin, were added by another hand in the first half of the eleventh century. The *Colloquy* is of interest as one of the earliest documents in the history of English education and for the picture it presents of the everyday life of the Anglo-Saxons.

1. **cildra** is a late form of the nom. pl. of *cild*, which would normally be *cildru* (§ 69 Note 2, § 117).

2. **tǣce :** subjunctive after verb of desiring (§ 235(*b*)).

3. **gewæmmodlice.** The *æ* results from front mutation ; the more usual form has *e* for *æ* (§ 40).

5. **rēce** 1 pl. pres. ind. The ending -*e* is used instead of -*aþ* when the verb is immediately followed by the pronoun (§ 158).

sprecan is a late form of the pres. subj. pl., earlier -*en* (§ 158).

6. **næs** is an emphatic adverb, ' not at all '.

8 f. **hit ne cunnan** is used to gloss Latin *nescire* and may best be translated ' be ignorant '.

12. **weorkes.** For the use of *k* as a spelling for *c*, cf. *geiukodan* 1. 26 and § 9.

13. **dæg** is a survival of an old locative without inflection.

14. **seofon tida.** The seven canonical ' hours ' were the main services of the monastic day. See note on ll. 65-74 and A. Hamilton Thompson, *English Monasteries*, pp. 136-140.

22. **yrþlincg** ' ploughman ', a derivative of *eorþe* ' earth ' (cf. 3.17). It is unlikely that the pupils did in fact follow all the occupations that are described in the *Colloquy*. The master assigned to each of the pupils a rôle and then questioned them in order to give them practice in the use of Latin.

24. **oxon** acc. pl. On the -*on* see § 112 Note 4.

hig is an inverted spelling for *hī* (§10).

24 f. **Nys hit** 'there is not'.

26 f. **geiukodan . . . syl.** Two dative absolutes corresponding to two ablative absolutes in the Latin. *gefæstnodon* is pl. because it refers to both *sceare* and *cultre*. On the endings -*an* and -*on* in the dat. pl. see § 118 Note 2.

34. **hig** is a noun ' hay ' ; *hig* is a pronoun ' them ' (see note on l. 24). In l. 35 *Hig* is an interjection.

40. **begyst**. The early WS. form was *begietst*. The *ts* was probably assimilated to *ss* (§ 90) and this was simplified before another consonant (§ 101). The *y* is a late WS. development of *ie*.

42. **fixas** from *fiscas* by metathesis (§ 92).

44. The Latin has *hamum* and the glossator was uncertain whether this meant *ancgil* ' hook ' or *ǣs* ' bait ' (see footnote).

wyrpe may be a spelling for *weorpe*, made possible by the fact that in late OE. both *wyr-* and *weor-* became *wur-* (§§ 59, 60).

spyrtan wicker pots to catch crabs and lobsters.

65-74. Some of the services referred to here are the ' hours ' mentioned in l. 14 : *ūhtsang* ' matins ', *prīm* ' prime ', *under(n)tīd* ' tierce ', *middæg* ' sext ', *nōn* ' none ', *ǣfen-(sangc)* ' vespers ', and *niht-sangc* ' compline '. In addition, certain supplementary devotions are mentioned.

66. **mīnon,** earlier *mīnum*, dat. sing. of the personal pronoun used as a possessive adjective.

70. **mæssan be dæge** Lat. *missam de die*, the mass for that particular day.

71. **sungan,** earlier *sungon*, 1 pl. pret. ind.

73. **gearuwe,** earlier *gearwe* (§ 76).

79. **āhsast** is an inverted spelling for *ācsast*, made possible by the change of *hs* to *cs* (spelt *x*) in such words as *weaxan* ' to grow '.

80. **ānra gehwylc** ' each one ' (§ 129).

81. **ytst**. The *y* is a late OE. spelling for *i*, which is from the *e* of *etan* by the raising of *e* to *i* in Germanic (§ 19).

82. Because he was so young, the boy was allowed to eat meat, which was forbidden to the monk.

85. **ǣigra**. The *i* is a glide before the palatal *g* and the final *-a* is a late OE. ending (cf. *cildra* l. 1) ; early OE. had *ǣgru*.

87. **etst**. The regular form would be *itst*, but *i* has been replaced by *e* on the analogy of such forms as the infinitive.

GLOSSARY

The Glossary serves also as an index to the Grammar. References to the Grammar are to paragraphs; other references are to extract and line of the prose texts.

The distinction between þ and ð is ignored, þ being used for both.

The order of words is alphabetical (æ following ad and þ following t).

Cross-references are generally given for forms occurring in the prose extracts but not for forms occurring only in the Grammar.

The gender of nouns is indicated by the abbreviations *m., f., n. (noun* is implied). The numbers after *sv.* and *wv.* refer to the classes of verbs in the Grammar.

ac *cj.* but 1. 39, 46.
āc *f.* oak § 113.
ǣ *f.* law (of God) 1. 52.
æcer *m.* field 3. 32, 5. 28 ; §§ 11, 74, 82.
æīen-glōmung *f.* twilight 2. 30.
ǣfen-(sangc) *m.* vespers 5. 74.
ǣfre *adv.* ever 1. 47.
æfter *prep. w. dat.* after 1. 39, 3. 8, according to 4. 76.
æfterra *comp. adj.* second § 128.
ǣg *n. ; pl.* ǣgru, ǣigra egg 5. 85 ; § 117.
ǣghwā *pron.* each one § 143.
ǣghwæþer, ǣgþer *pron.* each of two ; ǣgþer ge . . . ge both . . . and 1. 4, 7 ; § 143.
ǣghwilc *pron.* each one § 143.
ǣgþer *see* ǣghwæþer.
ǣht *f.* property 3. 7, 8.
ǣigra *see* ǣg.
ǣl *m.* eel 5. 55.
ǣlc *adj. pron.* each, every 1. 79, 80, 2. 18 ; § 145.
ǣlepūta *m.* eel-pout, burbot 5. 55.
ǣlmihtig *adj.* almighty 1. 21.
ǣni(g) *adj. pron.* any 1. 22, 5. 29 ; §§ 64, 89, 145.
ǣnne *see* ān.
æppel *m.* apple § 82.
æps, æspe *f.* aspen § 92.

ǣr, *prep. w. dat.* before 1. 69.
ǣr *adv.* formerly 1. 37, 4. 28 ; *superl.* ǣrest first 1. 52 ; § 126.
ærcebiscep *m.* archbishop 1. 75.
ǣrende *n.* message § 108.
ǣrendgewrit *n.* letter 1. 17.
ǣrendwreca *m.* messenger 1. 7.
ǣrra *adj. comp.* former ; *superl.* ǣrest(a) first §§ 126, 128.
ǣr-þǣm-þe *cj. w. subj.* before 1. 31.
æstel *m.* book-mark 1. 80 n, 82.
æt *prep. w. dat.* at, in 1. 85, from 1. 74.
ætforan *prep. w. dat.* before 5. 72.
ǣton *see* etan.
æþelborenness *f.* noble birth 4. 14, 18.
æþele *adj.* noble 2. 24 ; § 120.
āfeallan *sv.* 7 to decline 1. 69.
āfi(e)rran *wv.* 1 to remove § 40.
āfirsian *wv.* 2 to drive away, remove 4. 35.
āg *v.* I possess §§ 199, 210.
agen *prep. w. acc.* towards 3. 23.
āgen *adj.* own 1. 36, 46.
āhreddan *wv.* 1 to rescue § 193.
āhsian *see* āxian.
āhwā *pron.* anyone § 143.
āhwæþer *pron.* one of two § 143.
ald *see* eald.
ālȳfan *wv.* 1 to allow 4. 27

118

ālȳsan *wv.* 1 to deliver, set free 3. 5.

am *see* **bēon.**

āmyrran *wv.* 1 to waste 3. 42, to spend, squander 3. 11.

ān *adj. pron.* one, a single 1. 17, alone (*generally weak*) 4. 39 ; *acc. m.* **ānne, ǣnne** 1. 20, 4. 49 ; *f.* **āne** 1. 80; **ānra gehwylc** each one 5. 80 ; §§ 65, 128, 129, 145, 227.

ancgil *m.* fish-hook 5. 44.

and, ond *cj.* and 1. 2, 2. 2 ; § 64.

andgiet *n.* sense, understanding 1. 74 ; § 14.

andgitfullicost *adv. superl.* most intelligibly 1. 78.

andsaca *m.* adversary § 14.

andswarian, andswerian *wv.* 2 to answer 3. 38 ; § 193.

andweard *adj.* present 4. 57 ; § 118.

andwlita *m.* face 4. 6.

andwyrdan *wv.* 1 to answer 1. 47 ; § 194.

ānlēpe *adj.* single 1. 20.

ann *v.w. dat. gen.* I grant § 202.

ānne *see* **ān.**

ār *f.* honour §§ 69, 109.

ār *n.* copper 2. 20.

ārǣdan *wv.* 1 to read 1. 66, 70.

ārās *see* **ārīsan.**

ārecc(e)an *wv.* 1 ; 2 *sing. imper.* **ārece** ; *pret.* **āre(a)hte** to relate 4. 16, to expound, translate 1. 78.

ārfæst *adj.* virtuous § 118.

ārīsan *sv.* 1 ; *pret. sing.* **ārās** ; *pret. pl.* **ārison** to arise 3. 18, 21, 5. 72 ; § 165.

arn *see* **irnan.**

āseolcan *sv.* 3 to become sluggish § 32.

āstīgian *wv.* 2 to climb into 5. 43.

āstyrian, āstirian *wv.* 1 to move 3. 23, 4. 55.

āwendan *wv.* 1 to translate 1. 79.

āwiht, āht, ōht *pron.* anything ; **tō āhte** at all ; §§ 145, 150.

āwrītan *sv.* 1 to write, narrate 1. 36.

āxian, āxsian, āhsian *wv.* 2 to ask 3. 34, 4. 11, 5. 79 ; § 92.

bæcere *m.* baker 5. 21.

bæþ *n.*, *pl.* **baþo** bath, 2. 18.

bannan *sv.* 7 to summon § 190.

baþian *wv.* 2 to bathe § 13.

baþo *see* **bæþ.**

be, bi, big *prep. w. dat.* about, concerning 5. 67, by 4. 70, for 1. 73 ; *forming adv.* **be fullan** fully, completely 1. 45 ; **be sūþan** *prep. phrase w. dat.* south of 1. 20 ; **bī wrītan** to copy 1. 87 ; § 10.

bē(a)cen *n.* beacon § 53.

beadu *f.* battle §§ 76, 109.

bē(a)g, bēah *m.* ring, §§ 53, 85.

beald *adj.* bold § 106.

bealu *n.* evil § 108.

bēam *m.* tree § 12.

bēan *f.* bean 5. 85.

b(e)arn *n.* child § 33.

bearu *m.* grove §§ 87, 108.

bēatan *sv.* 7 to beat § 190.

bebēodan, bebīodan *sv.* 2 to command 1. 22, 81.

bebod *n.* command 3. 39 ; § 14.

bēc *see* **bōc.**

beclyppan *wv.* 1 to embrace 3. 24.

becuman *sv.* 4 ; *pret.* **becōm** to come 4. 3, to befall 1. 26.

bedd *n.* bed 5. 66.

befæstan *wv.* 1 to apply 1. 25.

befeolan *sv.* 3 to apply oneself 1. 64.

beforan *prep. w. dat.* before, in the presence of 3. 20, 25.

begān *v.* ; 2 *sing. pres.* **begǣst** to set about 5. 22.

begēaton *see* **begietan.**

bēgen *adj.* both § 130.

begietan *sv.* 5 ; 2 *sing. pres.* **begyst** ; *pret. pl.* **begēaton** to gain, obtain 1. 14, 38, 5. 40.

begiondan *prep. w. dat.* beyond 1. 19.

begyst *see* **begietan.**

behātan *sv.* 7 ; *pret. sing.* **behēt** to promise 4. 74.

behealdan *sv.* 7 to behold 2. 30.

behēfe *adj.* fitting, suitable 5. 6 ; § 14.

behēt *see* **behātan.**

eh ionan *prep. w. dat.* on this side bof 1.16.

belgan *sv.* 3 to become angry § 173.

benc *f.* bench § 13.

beneah *v.* it suffices § 208.

bēo *f.* bee § 112.

bēodan *sv.* 2 to command § 167.

bēon *v.* ; 1 *sing. pres.* eom ; 3 *sing. pres.* biþ, byþ to be 1. 80, 3. 20, 4. 79, 5. 75 ; §§ 155, 212, 213.

beorgan *sv.* 3 to protect § 32, 175.

bēorscipe *m.* feast 4. 64.

bepǣcan *wv.* 1 to deceive § 194.

beran *sv.* 4 to carry 4. 73 ; §§ 14, 19, 23, 25, 26, 70, 156, 157, 158, 160, 161, 177.

berende *ppl. adj. w. gen.*, productive 2. 9, 20.

berstan *sv.* 3 to burst §§ 35, 91, 171.

besēon *sv.* 5 ; *pret. sing.* beseah to look 4. 81.

besierwan *wv.* 1 to lie in wait for § 194.

besorgian *wv.* 2 *w. acc.* to sorrow for 4. 7.

beswin(c)gan *sv.* 3 ; *pp.* beswun(c)gen to beat 5. 7, 80.

bētan *wv.* 1 to make amends § 194.

bet(e)ra, betre, bet(e)st *see* gōd.

betwē(o)nan *adv.* from time to time 5. 15.

betwyh *prep. w. dat.* between 2. 2.

beþencan *wv.* 1 ; *pret.* beþōhte *reflex.* to consider 3. 16.

bewendan, bewǣndan *wv.* 1 *reflex.* to turn 4. 23.

bī *see* be.

bīdan *sv.* 1 to wait for § 164.

biddan *sv.* 5 to ask, bid 4. 79, to pray, beseech 4. 26 ; §§ 28, 90, 156, 157, 159, 160, 184.

bīen-codd *m.* bean-pod 3. 15.

big *see* be.

bigleofa *m.* livelihood, food 5. 41.

bigþ *see* bycgan.

bilewit *adj.* gentle, kind 5. 9.

bindan *sv.* 3 to bind §§ 18, 20, 101, 156, 157, 162, 172.

binne *f.* manger 5. 33.

birnan *sv.* 3 to burn § 172.

biscep *m.* bishop 1. 1, 75.

biscepstōl *m.* bishopric 1. 79.

bisgu *f.* occupation 1. 71.

bītan *sv.* 1 to bite § 164.

bit(t)er *adj.* bitter § 82.

biþ *see* bēon.

blæc *adj.* black 2. 21.

blǣcan *wv.* 1 to bleach 2. 16.

blǣdre, blæddre *f.* bladder § 104.

blandan *sv.* 7 to mingle § 189.

blāwan *sv.* 7 to blow § 190.

bledsian *wv.* 2 to bless § 65.

bliccet(t)an *wv.* 1 to glitter § 103.

blind *adj.* blind §§ 118, 122, 137.

blissian *wv.* 2 to rejoice 4. 32.

blīþe *adj.* joyful § 146 ; *adv.* joyfully, gladly 4. 69 ; § 146.

blōtan *sv.* 7 to sacrifice § 190.

blōwan *sv.* 7 to blossom § 190.

bōc *f.* ; *pl.* bēc book 1. 33, 45 ; §§ 13, 113.

bōcere *m.* scribe § 108.

bodian *wv.* 2 to proclaim § 196.

bōsm *m.* bosom § 13.

brād *adj.* broad 2. 5 ; § 124.

brǣmbel, brembel *m.* bramble §§ 65, 67.

brēadru *n. pl.* crumbs § 117.

brēaw, brēw, *m.* eyelid § 57.

brecan *sv.* 5 to break § 180.

bregdan, brēdan *sv.* 3 to brandish, to move quickly §§ 18, 32, 171.

bregu *m.* prince § 111.

bringan *wv.* 1 to bring 3. 27, 29 ; § 195.

brōc *f.* breeches § 113.

brōþor *m.* brother 3. 35, 45 ; § 115.

brūcan *sv.* 2 *w. dat.* to enjoy, eat 5. 82 ; §§ 40, 170.

bucca *m.* he-goat § 9.

būgan *sv.* 2 to bow § 170.

būr *m.* bower, room 4. 75.

burg, burh *f.* city, town §§ 13, 75, 85, 113.

burhsittende *adj.* town-dwelling 3. 13.

būtan, būton *prep. w. dat.* without, in addition to 2. 27 ; *cj. w. subj.* unless 1. 85.

butere *f.* butter 5. 85.

bycgan *wv.* 1 ; 3 *sing. pres.* bigþ to buy 5. 51 ; § 195.

bysgian *wv.* 2 to occupy, employ 5. 14.

bysig *adj.* busy §§ 70, 71, 119.

byþ *see* bēon.

cann *v.* ; *pl.* cunnon ; *pret.* cūþe I know, am able 1. 16, 5. 17 ; §§ 22, 199, 203.

capitolmæsse *f.* first mass 5. 69.

c(e)ald *adj.* cold § 27.

ce(a)lf *n.* calf 3. 36 ; § 117.

ceaster *f.* town, city 2. 25, 5. 50.

ceasterwara *m. pl.* citizens 5. 52.

celf *see* ce(a)lf.

ceorfan *sv.* 3 to cut, carve §§ 37, 53, 175.

cēosan *sv.* 2 to choose §§ 12, 13, 77, 79, 83, 84, 90, 110, 119, 168.

ciele *m.* cold § 36.

cild *n.* ; *pl.* cildru, cildra child 5. 1, 82 ; §§ 64, 117.

cinn *f.* chin § 83.

cinn *see* cynn.

cirice, cyrce *f.* church 1. 32, 5. 66.

clǣne *adj.* clean 5. 47, 86 ; *adv.* completely 1. 15 ; §§ 66, 124.

clǣnsian *wv.* 2 to cleanse § 66.

clēa *f.* ; *gen. dat. sing.* clawe claw §§ 27, 62, 93, 109.

clif *n.* cliff § 46.

climban *sv.* 3 to climb § 172.

clipian, cliopian, clypian *wv.* 2 to call, cry out 4. 57, to summon 3. 34 ; §§ 45, 73.

cnapa *m.* boy 5. 30.

cnāwan *sv.* 7 to know § 190.

cnēo(w) *n.* knee § 13.

cniht, cneoht *m.* boy, youth §§ 9, 50.

cnyll *m.* ringing of a bell 5. 65.

cōm *see* cuman.

coss *m.* kiss § 42.

costnung *f.* temptation 3. 5.

crabba *m.* crab 5. 62.

cræft *m.* skill 4. 55, 63.

crāwan *sv.* 7 to crow § 190.

Cristen *adj.* Christian 1. 29, 57.

cū *f.* cow § 113.

culter *m.* coulter 5. 27.

cuman *sv.* 4 ; 3 *sing. pres.* cymeþ; *pret.* cōm to come 1. 2, 2. 30 ; §§ 13, 23, 40, 93, 162, 179.

cunnon, cūþe ; cwǣdon, cwæþ *see* cann ; cweþan.

cweccan *wv.* 1 to shake § 195.

cwellan *wv.* 1 to kill § 195.

cwēn *f.* princess 4. 76.

cweorn *f.* mill § 111.

cweþan *sv.* 5 ; *pret. sing.* cwæþ ; *pret. pl.* cwǣdon to say 1. 36, 47, 4. 4 ; § 182.

5*

cwic *adj.* alive §§ 59, 118.

cȳdde *see* cȳþan.

cyld *f.* cold 5. 31.

cymeþ *see* cuman.

cynehelm *m.* crown 4. 49.

cyning(c), kyning, cyng(c) *m.* king 1. 1, 4. 1, 2, 5, 22 ; §§ 72, 100.

cynn, cinn *n.* kind, kin, race 2. 7, 12 ; §§ 11, 52, 83.

cȳpan *wv.* 1 to sell 5. 49.

cȳpmann *m.* merchant 5. 20.

cyrce *see* cirice.

cyre *f.* choice §§ 77, 110.

cȳse *m.* cheese 5. 85 ; § 44.

cyssan *wv.* 1 to kiss 3. 24, 4. 2 ; §§ 13, 42, 101, 194.

cyst *f.* choice § 110.

cȳþan *wv.* 1 ; *pret.* cȳdde to make known 1. 2 ; §§ 90, 194.

dǣd *f.* deed § 110.

dæg, dæi *m.* ; *pl.* dagas day 2. 32, 5. 13, dæges by day §§ 113, 149, 225 ; §§ 13, 27, 71, 79, 89, 105, 108, 156.

dægrǣd *n.* daybreak 5. 24.

dægredlic *adj.* morning 5. 68.

dæi *see* dæg.

dǣl *m.* part 1. 46, share 3. 7.

dǣlan *wv.* 1 to divide, share 3. 8.

dagas *see* dæg.

dēad *adj.* dead 3. 30, 45.

dēag *v.* I avail §§ 199, 201.

deagung *f.* daybreak, dawn 2. 31.

dear(r) *v.* ; *pres. subj.* durre, dyrre I dare 5. 25, 79 ; §§ 199, 205.

dehter *see* dohtor.

delfan *sv.* 3 to dig § 173.

dēman *wv.* 1 to judge §§ 11, 40, 72, 95, 194, 199.

Dene *m. pl.* Danes § 110.

deorfan *sv.* 3 to work 5. 23.

dēorwurþe *adj.* valuable 4. 71.

derian *wv.* 1 to injure § 193.

dēst, dēþ *see* dōn.

dīgol *n.* secret 5. 80.

dōgor *n.* day §§ 117, 156.

dohtor *f.* ; *dat. sing.* dehter daughter 4. 2, 23 ; §§ 40, 41, 115.

dōm *m.* judgement § 40.

dōn *v.* ; 2 *sing. pres.* **dēst** ; *3 sing.* **dēþ** ; 2 *sing. pret.* **dydest** to do, perform 1. 12, to act 4.40, to make 3. 21, to put, place 1. 68, to remove 1. 82 ; §§ 212, 214.

dreccan *wv.* 1 to afflict § 195.

drencan *wv.* 1 to give to drink § 194.

drēosan *sv.* 2 to fall § 168.

drepan *sv.* 5 to strike § 180.

drincan *sv.* 3 ; *pret. pl.* **druncon** to drink 5. 71 ; §§ 18, 172.

drohtnian *wv.* 2 to live 5. 83.

druncon *see* **drincan.**

dryhten, drihten *m.* lord §§ 52, 108.

dūfan *sv.* 2 to dive § 170.

durre *see* **dear(r).**

duru *f.* door § 111.

dwellan *wv.* 1 to hinder § 195.

dydest *see* **dōn.**

dynnan *wv.* 1 to make a noise § 193.

dysi(g) *adj.* foolish §§ 10, 64.

ēa *f.* river 5. 43.

ēac *adv.* also, moreover 1. 9, 57 ; **ēac swylce, swylce ēac** likewise 2. 9, 5. 19.

ēage *n.* eye 4. 22 ; §§ 54, 112.

e(a)hta *num.* eight 2. 4 ; §§ 13, 53, 128.

eahtatēoþa *num.* eighteenth § 128.

eahtatīene *num.* eighteen § 128.

eahtoþa *num.* eighth § 128.

ēalā *interj.* oh ! alas ! 3. 16, 5. 1.

eald, ald *adj. ;* *comp.* **ieldra, yldra, ældra, eldra ;** *superl.* **ieldest** old, former 4. 26 ; **yldran** *m. pl.* ancestors 1. 37 ; §§ 27, 33, 40, 44, 51, 124.

eall *adj. pron.* all 1. 12, 31, 4. 57 ; §§ 102, 118, 227 ; *adv.* altogether § 149 ; **ealles** *adv.* altogether § 225 ; **mid ealle** altogether § 150.

eallunga *adv.* altogether § 148.

ealneg *adv.* always 1. 85 ; § 14, 149.

ēalond *n.* island 2. 1, 6.

ealu *n.* ale §§ 47, 114.

eardian *wv.* 2 to inhabit § 196.

ēare *n.* ear § 112.

earm *adj.* poor, wretched, miserable 4. 80 ; § 124.

earme *adv.* miserably § 152.

eart *see* **bēon.**

ēast *adv.* ; *comp.* **ēasterra ;** *superl.* **ēastmest** eastwards § 127.

ēaþe *adv.* ; *comp.* **īeþ** easily 1. 61 ; § 153.

Ēbrēisc *adj.* Hebrew 1. 52.

ednīwian *wv.* 2 to renew 4. 25.

efn *adj.* even § 90.

efnan, æfnan *wv.* 1 to perform § 40.

efne *adv.* indeed 3. 39.

eft *adv.* afterwards 1. 46, 53.

ege *m.* fear 5. 25.

ehta *see* **e(a)hta.**

el(n)boga *m.* elbow § 97.

elne *adv.* vigorously § 149.

ende *m.* end, conclusion 4. 22.

en(d)le(o)fan *num.* eleven § 128.

en(d)le(o)fta *num.* eleventh § 128.

Englisc *adj.* English 1. 66, English language 1. 18 ; § 70.

ēode, eom *see* **gān, bēon.**

eornostlīce *adv.* indeed § 147.

eorþe *f.* earth 3. 2, land, country 2. 9 ; § 13.

ēow(er) *see* **gē.**

eowestre *m.* sheepfold § 56.

erian *wv.* 1 to plough 5. 27 ; § 3.

etan *sv.* 5 ; 2 *sing. pres.* **etst, ytst ;** *pret. pl.* **ǣton** to eat 3. 15, 30, 5. 84, 87 ; § 180.

ēþel *m.* territory 1. 9.

fæc *n.* space, interval 2. 4.

fæder *m.* ; *gen. sing.* **fæder** father 3. 1, 17, 4. 28 ; § 115.

fǣge *adj.* fated § 120.

fægen *adj.* glad §§ 119, 122.

fæger *adj.* fair, beautiful 2. 17, 4. 59 ; §§ 13, 27.

fǣringa, fǣrunga *adv.* suddenly 4. 1 ; § 148.

fæs(t)nian *wv.* 2 to fasten 5. 26 ; § 97.

fæt *n.* ; *pl.* **f(e)atu** vessel §§ 27, 47, 108.

fǣt(t) *adj.* fat 3. 29, 36.

fæþm *m.* embrace § 84.

fagc *f.* plaice 5. 62.

fāh *adj.* hostile § 118.

fangen *see* **fōn.**

faran *sv.* 6 to go 3. 18 ; §§ 40, 41, 47, 185.

fealdan *sv.* 7 to fold §§ 106, 190.

feallan *sv.* 7 ; *pret. pl.* **fēollon** to fall 4. 22 ; § 190.

fearh, færh *m.* pig § 54.

fēa(we), fēawa *adj.* few 1. 16, 19 ; §§ 121, 227.

feccan *wv.* 1 to fetch 4. 34, 36.

fēdan *wv.* 1 to feed §§ 66, 194.

fēhst *see* **fōn**.

fela *adj. indecl. w. gen. pl.* many 3. 17, 5. 63.

feld *m.* field 5. 24 ; § 111.

fēng *see* **fōn**.

fēog(e)an *wv.* 1 to hate § 9.

feoh *n.* money 5. 41.

feohtan *sv.* 3 to fight §§ 32, 40, 50, 175.

feolan *sv.* 3 to penetrate, enter §§ 32, 173.

fēollon *see* **feallan**.

fēond, fīond *m.* enemy §§ 12, 63, 95, 116.

feorh *n.* life § 108.

feorlen *adj.* distant 3. 10.

feorr *adv. adj. ; comp.* **fyrra** far 3. 22 ; § 40, 124, 126, 151, 153.

feorran *adv.* from afar § 151.

fēower *num.* four 4. 70 ; § 128.

fēowertēoþa *num.* fourteenth § 128.

fēowertīene *num.* fourteen § 128.

fēowertig *num.* forty § 128.

fēowertigoþa *num.* fortieth § 128.

fēo(we)rþa *num.* fourth § 128.

fēran *wv.* 1 to go, travel 3. 9, 12.

feter *f.* fetter § 156.

fīf *num.* five §§ 96, 128.

fīfta *num.* fifth § 128.

fīftēoþa *num.* fifteenth § 128.

fīftīene *num.* fifteen § 128.

fīftig *num.* fifty 1. 81 ; § 128.

fīftigoþa *num.* fiftieth § 128.

findan *sv.* 3 ; *pp.* **funden** to find 1. 53 ; § 172.

fiorm *f.* use 1. 34.

firen *f.* crime §§ 69, 109.

first *m.* time 1. 65.

fisc *m.* ; *pl.* **fiscas, fixas** fish 5. 46, 85 ; §§ 13, 92.

fiscere *m.* fisherman 5. 19, 39.

fiscian, fixian *wv.* 2 to fish 5. 57.

fiscwylle *adj.* rich in fish 2. 10.

fixas, fixian *see* **fisc, fiscian**.

flǣscmete *m.* meat 5. 82.

flēan *sv.* 6 to flay § 186.

flēon *sv.* 2 to flee 2. 22 ; §§ 40, 169.

flōc *n.* fluke, flounder 5. 62.

flōr *f.* floor § 111.

flōwan *sv.* 7 to flow §§ 57, 190.

folc *n.* people, nation 1. 6, 4. 60.

folgian *wv.* 2 to follow 3. 13.

fōn *sv.* 7 ; *2 sing. pres.* **fēhst** ; *pret. sing.* **fēng** ; *pp.* (ge)**fangen** to seize, catch 2. 11, 5. 60 ; **tō rīce fēng** came to the throne 1. 21 ; §§ 3, 21, 63, 77, 78, 189.

for *prep. w. dat.* for 5. 25, on account of 1. 26, for the sake of 5. 8 ; **for hwī** why 5. 57.

forbærnan *wv.* 1 to burn 1. 31.

forbēodan *sv.* 2 to forbid § 162.

ford *m.* ford § 111.

fore *adv.* before §§ 126, 127.

forgiefan, forgyfan *sv.* 5 ; *pret. sing.* **forgeaf** to forgive 3. 4, to give 4. 84.

forgiefen(n)es *f.* forgiveness § 103.

forgietan *sv.* 5 to forget § 181.

forgyfan *see* **forgiefan**.

forgȳman *wv.* 1 to neglect, disregard 3. 40.

forhergian *wv.* 2 to ravage 1. 31.

forlǣtan *sv.* 7 ; *pret. sing.* **forlēt** ; *pl.* **forlēton** to leave, relinquish 4. 58, to lose 1. 40, to neglect 1. 49.

forlēosan *sv.* 2 ; *pret. sing.* **forlēas** to lose 4. 17 ; § 168.

forlēt(on) *see* **forlǣtan**.

forliden *ppl. adj.* shipwrecked 4. 8.

forma *adj. superl.* first §§ 127, 128.

formest(a) *adj. superl.* first §§ 127, 128, 134.

forspillan *wv.* 1 to squander 3. 10.

forstandan *sv.* 6 ; *pret. sing.* **forstōd** to understand 1. 78.

forþ *adv.* forth 4. 59 ; § 126.

for-þām, for-þǣm, for-þon *cj.* for, because 3. 30, 5. 58 ; *adv.* therefore 1. 22, 40.

for-þām-þe, for-þǣm-þe, for-þan-þe *cj.* because 1. 34, 2. 27, 3. 36.

for-þȳ *adv.* therefore 1. 84, accordingly 1. 58.

forwandigende *ppl. adj.* hesitating 4. 13.

forweorþan, forwurþan *sv.* 3 ; *pret. sing.* **forwearþ** to perish 3. 18, 31, 46.

fōt *m.* ; *pl.* **fēt** foot 3. 29 ; §§ 68, 113, 156.

fox *m.* fox § 42.

fracod *adj.* worthless 5. 6.

frætuwe *f. pl.* trappings § 76.

fram, from *prep. w. dat.* from 1. 82, 2. 5, by 4. 27.

fram *adj.* bold § 40.

frēa *m.* lord § 112.

fremman, fræmman *wv.* 1 to perform §§ 40, 193.

frēo(h), frīo *adj.* free 1. 63, 5. 37.

frēond *m.* ; *pl.* **frȳnd** friend 3. 41, 4.34 ; § 116.

frēondlīce *adv.* in a friendly manner 1. 2 ; § 147.

frēosan *sv.* 2 to freeze § 168.

fretan *sv.* 5 to devour § 180.

fricgan *sv.* 5 to ask § 184.

frignan *sv.* 3 to ask §§ 64, 162, 172.

frīo *see* **frēo(h)**.

frogga *m.* frog § 13.

from *see* **fram** *prep.*

frȳnd *see* **frēond**.

fugelere *m.* fowler 5. 20.

fugol *m.* bird 2. 10 ; §§ 13, 55, 74.

full *adj. w. gen.* full 5. 27 ; **be fullan** fully, completely 1. 45 ; § 55.

ful(l) *adv.* completely § 149.

fultum *m.* help 1. 62.

funden *see* **findan**.

furh *f.* furrow §§ 13, 113.

furþor, furþur *adv.* further 1. 67.

furþra *adj. comp.* superior § 126.

furþum *adv.* even 1. 17, 20.

fūs *adj.* eager § 40.

fyl(i)gan *wv.* 1 to follow § 75.

fyllan *wv.* 1 *w. gen.* to fill 1. 33, 5. 33 ; § 194.

fȳr *n.* fire 2. 22.

fyrd *f.* English army § 4.

fyrest(a) *adj. superl.* first §§ 126, 128, 134.

fyrmest(a) *adj. superl.* first §§ 127, 128, 134.

fyrra *see* **feorr**.

fȳsan *wv.* 1 to send forth § 40.

fyxen *f.* vixen § 42.

gād *n.* lack § 87.

gādīsen *n.* iron goad 5. 30.

gǣlsa *m.* wantonness, pride 3. 11.

gærs *n.* grass § 91.

gagates *m.* agate 2. 21.

galan *sv.* 6 to sing § 185.

gān *v.* ; *pret. sing.* **ēode** to go 3. 37, to come 4. 2 ; §§ 40, 212, 215.

gangan *sv.* 7 to go, walk § 190.

gārsecg *m.* sea, ocean 2. 1.

gāt *f.* goat § 113.

ge *cj.* and 1. 4, 7, 8.

gē *pron.* you 4. 81 ; §§ 136, 137.

gēa *adv.* yes 5. 36.

geǣmetigian *wv.* 2 *w. acc. gen.* to free 1. 24.

geanwyrde *adj.* professed 5. 13.

gē(a)r *n.* year 3. 39 ; §§ 38, 53.

geāra *adv.* long ago § 149.

gearu *adj.* ready 5. 73 ; §§ 3, 86, 121, 122, 146.

gearwe *adv.* completely § 146.

geat *n.* gate 2. 26.

gebelgan *sv.* 3 ; *pret. sing.* **gebealh** *reflex.* to become angry 3. 37.

gebēorscipe *m.* feast 4. 10, 77.

geblissian *wv.* 2 to rejoice 3. 44.

gebrōþru *m. pl.* brothers 5. 14, 67.

gebyrian *wv.* 1 to befit 3. 44, to belong 3. 8.

gecīgan *wv.* 1 to call, summon 4. 34.

gecnāwan *sv.* 7 to understand 1. 61.

gecwǣþ *see* **gecweþan**.

gecwēman *wv.* 1 to please 4. 8.

gecweþan *sv.* 5 ; *pret.* **gecwǣþ** to say 4. 1.

gedæghwāmlic *adj.* daily 3. 3.

gedafenian *wv.* 2 to be fitting 4. 12.

gedeorf *n.* labour, trouble 5. 35, 36.

gedōn *v.* to do 4. 28 ; to make 4. 30, to bring it about 1. 61.

geedcucian *wv.* 2 to come to life 3. 31, 45.

geendian *wv.* 2 to come to an end 4. 77.

geendung *f.* end 4. 64.

gefangen *see* **fōn**.

gefeallan *sv.* 7 ; *pret. sing.* **gefēol** to apply onself 4. 64, to come by chance 4. 43.

gefēhst *see* **gefōn**.

gefeoht *n.* fight § 50.

gefēol *see* **gefeallan**.

gefēon *sv.* 5 to rejoice §§ 183, 184.

gefēra *m.* companion 5. 17, 29.

geflit n. dispute 2. 30.
gefōn sv. 7 ; 2 sing. pres. **gefēhst** to catch 5. 42, 52.
gefrignan sv. 3 to learn §§ 99, 162.
gefyllan wv. 1 to fill 3. 15.
gegaderian wv. 2 to gather together 3. 9.
gegyrla m. dress, clothing 3. 27.
gehæftan wv. 1 to confine, imprison 5. 44.
gehālgod see **hālgian**.
gehealdan sv. 7 ; pret. pl. **gehīoldon** to preserve 1. 8.
gehī(e)ran, gehīoldon see **gehȳran, gehealdan**.
gehwā pron. each one § 143.
gehwæþer pron. each of two § 143.
gehwilc, gehwylc pron. each ; **ānra gehwylc** each person 5. 80 ; §§ 129, 143.
gehȳran, gehī(e)ran wv. 1 to hear 3. 33 ; § 162.
geiukod see **iucian**.
gelædan wv. 1 to lead 3. 5.
gelæred ppl. adj. learned 1. 83.
gelæstan wv. 1 to carry out § 194.
gelaþian wv. 2 to invite 4. 9.
gelī(e)fan wv. 1 to believe 1. 23.
geliornian wv. 2 to learn 1. 53, 55.
gelymp n. adventure 4. 21, event, misfortune 4. 16.
gemǣne adj. common § 14.
gemǣngan wv. 1 to join, blend, mingle 4. 37, 56.
geman v. ; pret. **gemunde** I remember 1. 30, 68 ; § 207.
gemēt(ed) see **mētan**.
gemiltsigend m. pitier 4. 80.
gemunde see **geman**.
gemynd nf. mind, memory 1. 3.
gemyne adj. mindful § 120.
genam see **geniman**.
geneah v. it suffices § 208.
genēalǣcan wv. 1 w. dat. to approach 3. 33.
genemned see **nemnan**.
genesan sv. 5 to be saved § 182.
genihtsum adj. abundant 2. 15.
geniman sv. 4 ; pret. sing. **genam** to take, seize, catch 4. 54, to take away 5. 45.
genōg, genōh adj. enough 3. 17 ; §§ 118, 227.

geō, (g)iū adv. formerly 1. 3, 44, 2. 24 ; §§ 13, 83.
geoc n. yoke § 38.
geolu adj. yellow § 121.
geōmor adj. sad § 119.
geong, iung adj. ; comp. **gingra** ; superl. **gingest** young 3. 6, 9 ; as sb. young man 4. 35 ; §§ 13, 38, 83, 124.
georn, giorn adj. willing, eager 1. 11 ; §§ 37, 146.
georne adv. willingly § 146.
gēotan sv. 2 to pour § 167.
gerestan wv. 1 to rest 4. 85.
gerȳman wv. 1 to extend 1. 9.
gesǣliglic adj. happy 1. 4.
gesāwon see **gesēon**.
gesceaft f. creation § 14.
gescrǣpe adj. fit, suitable 2. 8, 19.
gescȳ n. pair of shoes 3. 28.
gesēon, gesīon sv. 5 ; pret. sing. **geseah** ; pl. **gesāwon** to see 1. 31, 39, 4. 14, 77.
gesettan wv. 1 to set, place 2. 2.
gesi(e)hþ f. sight § 54.
gesingian, gesyngian wv. 2. to sin, offend 4. 24.
gesion see **gesēon**.
gesittan sv. 5 to sit, take possession of §§ 84, 162.
gesthūs n. inn, lodging 4. 84.
gestrēon n. property § 40.
gesund adj. safe, well 4. 79.
gesyllan, gesellan wv. 1 to sell 5. 53.
getogen see **tēon** sv. 2.
geþencean wv. 1 to think 1. 26, to think of 1. 20.
geþēode, geþīode n. language 50.
gewæmmodlīce adv. corruptly 5. 3.
gewendan, gewǣndan wv. 1 to go 4. 79, to turn 4. 4.
geweorþan, gewurþan sv. 3 to be fulfilled 3. 2.
gewiht n. weight 4. 71.
gewilnian wv. 2 to wish 3. 14.
gewislīce, gewyslīce adv. certainly, plainly 4. 20, indeed 5. 33.
gewistfullian, gewystfullian wv. 2 to feast 3. 30, 41, 44.
gewistlǣcan wv. 1 to feast, make merry 3. 32.
gewītan sv. 1 to depart § 164.

geworden *see* weorþan.
geworht *see* wyrcan.
gewrit *n.* writing, document 1. 66.
gewurþan *see* geweorþan.
gewyslīce, gewystfullian *see* gewislīce, gewistfullian.
gi(e)fan, gyfan *sv.* 5 to give 4. 26,
   66 ; §§ 12, 13, 36, 51, 77, 83, 85,
   181.
gi(e)fu *f.* gift 4. 76; § 109.
gieldan *sv.* 3 to pay §§ 36, 174.
giellan *sv.* 3 to yell § 174.
gielpan *sv.* 3 to boast § 174.
gierwan *wv.* 1 to prepare §§ 93, 194.
giest *m.* stranger § 68.
gī(e)t, gȳt *adv.* still, yet 1. 39, 3. 22,
   4. 45.
gif *cj. w. ind. or subj.* if 1. 14, 4. 11,
   15, whether 5. 80.
gifan, gifu *see* gi(e)fan, gi(e)fu.
gimm, gym *m.* gem 2. 22.
gingra, gingest *see* geong.
gioguþ *f.* youth, young men 1. 63.
giond *prep. w. acc.* throughout
   1. 3, 5.
giorn *see* georn.
git *pron.* you two §§ 136, 137.
gīt *see* gī(e)t.
giū *see* geō.
glæd *adj.* ; *superl.* gladost glad §§
   13, 118, 124.
glēaw *adj.* wise § 121.
god *m.* God 1. 6, 12, *n.* heathen god
   4. 53 ; § 11.
gōd *adj.* good 1. 44, 4. 4 ; *comp.*
   bet(e)ra, *superl.* bet(e)st §§ 11, 13,
   118, 125.
godcund *adj.* religious 1. 4, 10.
gōddōnd *m.* benefactor § 116.
godspell *n.* gospel § 65.
gold *n.* gold 4. 70 ; §§ 42, 106.
goldhord *n.* treasury 4. 67.
gōs *f.* ; *pl.* gēs goose §§ 13, 22, 113.
grēat *adj.* ; *comp.* grīetra, *superl.*
   grīetest great § 124.
Greccas *m. pl.* Greeks 1. 53.
grēne *adj.* green § 11.
grētan *wv.* 1 to greet 1. 1, 4. 78.
grōwan *sv.* 7 to grow 2. 9 ; § 190.
grūt *f.* coarse meal § 113.
guma *m.* man § 112.
gyfan *see* gi(e)fan.
gylden *adj.* golden §§ 42, 70, 119.

gylt *m.* guilt, offence 3. 4.
gyltend *m.* offender 3. 4.
gym *see* gimm.
gyrd *f.* rod 5. 83.
gȳt *see* gī(e)t.

habban *wv.* 3 ;   2 *sing. pres.*
   hæfst, hafast ; 3 *sing.* hæfþ ;
   pret. hæfde to have 1. 14, 22,
   5. 11 ; §§ 11, 13, 197.
hacod *m.* pike (fish) 5. 55.
hād *m.* rank, order 1. 4, position
   1. 68, condition, sex 2. 19.
hæbbe(n), hæfde, hæfdon, hæfst,
   hæfþ *see* habban.
hǣlan *wv.* 1 to heal § 40.
hæle *m.* man § 114.
hǣlend *m.* Saviour § 116.
hæleþ *m.* man § 114.
hǣrincg *m.* herring 5. 61.
hǣs *f.* command 4. 76.
hǣþen *adj. as sb.* heathen 4. 52.
hafast, hafaþ *see* habban.
hāl *adj.* safe, whole 3. 36 ; § 40.
hālga *m.* saint 5. 68.
hālgian *wv.* 2 ; *pp.* gehālgod to
   hallow, sanctify 3. 1.
hālig *adj.* holy §§ 72, 119, 122, 123,
   137.
hām *m.* home 4. 79, 5. 25 ; §§ 11, 66.
hām-stede *m.* homestead § 66.
hand *f.* hand 3. 28, 4. 50 ; §§ 69,
   111.
hās *adj.* hoarse 5. 31.
hāt *adj.* hot 2. 18.
hātan *sv.* 7 ; *pret.* hēt to command,
   bid 1. 1, 4. 36, to call 2. 2 ;
   §§ 155, 157, 188, 189, 233.
hē *pron.* he, it 4. 7 ; þe his whose ;
   þe him to whom §§ 64, 136, 230.
hēafod *n.* head 4. 49 ; §§ 69, 108.
hēah *adj.* ; *comp.* hīehra, hīerra;
   superl. hīehst high 1. 68 ; §§ 63,
   90, 118, 124.
healdan *sv.* 7 ; *pret.* hēold, hīold
   to hold, occupy 1. 37, to tend
   3. 14, *reflex.* to behave 5. 77 ;
   § 190.
heall *f.* hall 4. 54.
hēan *wv.* 1 to exalt § 194.
heard *adj.* hard § 12.
hearpe *f.* harp 4. 34, 36.

hearpenægl *m.* plectrum 4. 54.
hearpestreng *m.* harp-string 4. 55.
hearpian *wv.* 2 to play on the harp 4. 36.
hēawan *sv.* 7 to hew § 190.
hebban *sv.* 6 to raise §§ 81, 187.
hefig *adj.* heavy, severe 4. 15.
helan *sv.* 4 to conceal § 177.
helpan *sv.* 3 ; *pp.* **holpen** to help §§ 18, 19, 20, 32, 119, 156, 173.
hēo, hīo *pron.* she, it 1. 15 ; § 136.
heofon, heofen *m.* heaven 3. 1, 25 ; §§ 45, 72, 73.
hēold *see* **healdan.**
heolstor, helustr *m.* darkness § 45.
heom, heora *see* **hīe.**
heorot *m.* hart § 45.
heoru *m.* sword § 111.
hēr *adv.* here 1. 38, 50 ; § 151.
here *m.* invading army §§ 4, 40, 88.
hergian *wv.* 2 to harry, ravage § 4.
herian *wv.* 1 to praise 4. 38, 40 ; § 79.
hēt *see* **hātan.**
hī *see* **hīe.**
hider, hieder *adv.* here ; **hieder on lond** here in this land 1. 13 ; §§ 10, 151.
hīe, hī, hig *pron.* they, them 5. 34 ; §§ 10, 45, 136.
hieder *see* **hider.**
hiene, hiera *see* **hē, hīe.**
hī(e)ran, hȳran, hēran *wv.* 1 to hear §§ 12, 40, 51, 162.
hierde *m.* shepherd § 108.
hierdebōc *f.* shepherd's book 1. 73.
hiere *see* **hēo.**
hierra *see* **hēah.**
hig *interj.* O ! 5. 35.
hīg *n.* hay 5. 34.
hig *see* **hīe.**
him *see* **hē, hit, hīe.**
hindema *adj. superl.* hindmost, last § 127.
hine, hīo *see* **hē, hēo.**
hīold(on) *see* **healdan.**
hionan *adv.* from here § 151.
hiora, hira *see* **hīe.**
hire *see* **hēo.**
his *see* **hē, hit.**
hit *pron.* it 1. 31 ; § 136.
hīw *n.* colour 2. 14.
hlāf *m.* bread 3. 3, 17.

hlāford *m.* lord, master 5. 23, 26 ; §§ 94, 108.
hlēapan *sv.* 7 to run § 190.
hli(e)hhan *sv.* 6 to laugh §§ 13, 40, 81, 187.
hlūd *adj.* loud § 13.
hnesce *adj.* soft § 13.
hnitu *f.* nit § 113.
hnutu *f.* nut § 113.
hōlunga *adv.* without cause § 148.
hōn *sv.* 7 to hang § 189.
hors *n.* horse § 91.
hrēam *m.* noise, shouting 5. 31.
hrēosan *sv.* 2 to fall § 168.
hring *m.* ring 3. 28 ; § 13.
hrīþer *n.* cow, ox, *pl.* cattle § 117.
hron *m.* whale 2. 11.
hrōpan *sv.* 7 to shout § 190.
hrycg *m.* back § 13.
hū *adv.* how 1. 4, 7, 9.
hūlic *pron.* of what kind § 142.
hund *n. w. gen.* hundred 2. 4 ; §§ 64, 128, 133.
hundeahtatig *num.* eighty § 128.
hundeahtatigoþa *num.* eightieth § 128.
hundendlefontig *num.* one hundred and ten § 128.
hundendleftigoþa *num.* hundred and tenth § 128.
hundnigontig *num.* ninety § 128.
hundnigontigoþa *num.* ninetieth § 128.
hundred *n.* hundred §§ 64, 128.
hundseofontig *num.* seventy § 128.
hundseofontigoþa *num.* seventieth § 128.
hundtēontig *num.* hundred § 128.
hundtēontigoþa *num.* hundredth § 128.
hundtwelftig *num.* one hundred and twenty § 128.
hundtwelftigoþa *num.* hundred and twentieth § 128.
hungor, hunger *m.* hunger 3. 12, 18; § 13.
hunig, huneg *n.* honey § 71.
hunta *m.* hunter 5. 19.
hūs *n.* house 3. 17, 33 ; §§ 11, 13.
hwā *pron. interr.* who 5. 51 ; *indef.* anyone 1. 87 ; **swā hwā swā** whoever : **nāt hwā** someone ; §§ 64, 141, 143, 144.

hwænne *adv. interr.* when 5. 74.

hwǣr *adv.* where 5. 49, anywhere 1. 86 ; § 151.

hwæt *adj.* bold § 118.

hwæt *pron. interr.* ; *instr.* **hwī, hwȳ, hwon** what 4. 5 ; *adv.* why 5. 79 ; §§ 13, 141 ; **swā hwæt swā, lōc hwæt** whatever § 144 ; **nāt hwæt** something § 144.

hwæthwugu *pron.* something § 143.

hwæþer *pron.* which of two ; **swā hwæþer swā, lōc hwæþer** whichever §§ 142, 143, 144 ; *cj. w. ind. or subj.* whether 2. 30.

hwanon, hwonan *adv.* whence 4. 10 ; § 151.

hwelc, hwilc, hwylc *adj. pron.* what, what sort of 1. 3, 5. 38, 54; §§ 58, 142, 143 ; **swā hwelc swā** whichever § 144 ; **nāt hwelc** someone § 144.

hwelchwugu *pron.* someone § 143.

hwettan *wv.* 1 to incite § 193.

hwī *see* **hwæt** *pron.*

hwider *adv.* whither § 151.

hwīl *f.* space of time ; **þā hwīle þe** so long as 1. 65.

hwilc *see* **hwelc.**

hwīlum, hwīlon *adv.* sometimes, 1. 73, 5. 58 ; § 149.

hwītra, hwittra *adj. comp.* whiter § 104.

hwon *see* **hwæt** *pron.*

hwonan *see* **hwanon.**

hwōpan *sv.* 7 to threaten § 190.

hwȳ *see* **hwæt** *pron.*

hwylc *see* **hwelc.**

hȳ *see* **hēo, hīe.**

hycg(e)an *wv.* 3 to think § 197.

hȳdan *wv.* 1 to hide § 11.

hyne *see* **hē.**

hyngran *wv.* 1 to be hungry §§ 72, 194.

hyre *see* **hēo.**

hȳrsumian *wv.* 1 to obey 1. 7.

hys, hyt *see* **hē.**

ic *pron.* ; *acc. and dat.* **mē** ; *gen.* **mīn** I 1. 18, 19 ; §§ 136, 137, 227.

īdel *adj.* idle, empty 5. 6.

īecan *wv.* 1 to increase § 194.

ielde *m. pl.* men § 110.

ielfe *m. pl.* elves § 110.

ierre, iorre, eorre *adj.* angry § 40.

īl, igil *m.* hedgehog §§ 64, 89.

ilca *adj.* same §§ 140, 227.

in(n) *adv.* in, inside 3. 37 ; § 151.

innan, innon *adv.* within, from within ; *prep. w. dat.* inside 4. 53, 74 ; § 151.

innanbordes *adv.* at home 1. 8 ; § 149.

inne *adv.* within §§ 127, 151.

innemest *adj. superl.* inmost § 127.

innon *see* **innan.**

īow(er) *see* **gē.**

irnan *sv.* 3 ; *pret. sing.* **arn** to run 3. 24 ; §§ 35, 172.

is *see* **bēon.**

īsern *n.* iron 2. 20.

iū *see* **geō.**

iucian *wv.* 2 ; *pp.* **geiukod** to yoke 5. 24, 26.

iūgeāra *adv.* formerly 2. 1.

iung *see* **geong.**

kynerīce *n.* kingdom 1. 71.

kyning *see* **cyning(c).**

lācan *sv.* 7 to move, play §§ 188, 189.

Lǣden *n.* the Latin language 1. 18.

Lǣdengeþīode *n.* the Latin language 1. 67.

Lǣdenware *m. pl.* Romans 1. 55.

lǣfan *wv.* 1 to leave 1. 38.

lǣn *f.* loan 1. 86.

lǣran *wv.* 1 to teach 1. 66, 67 ; § 194.

lǣs *f.* ; *dat. sing.* **lǣswe** pasture 2. 8.

lǣs *see* **lȳt.**

lǣssa *see* **lȳtel.**

lǣst *see* **lȳt, lȳtel.**

lǣt *adj.* ; *superl.* **lǣtest, lǣtemest** late § 127.

lǣtan, lētan *sv.* 7 to allow §§ 188, 189.

lāgon *see* **licgan.**

lagu *m.* sea § 111.

lamb *n.* lamb § 117.

lamprede *f.* lamprey 5. 56.

land, lond *n.* land, country 1. 13, 50, 2. 17 ; § 24.

lang *adj ;* *comp.* lengra ; *superl.* lengest long 2. 4, 32 ; §§ 13, 124.

lange, longe *adv. ;* *comp.* leng ; *superl.* lengest long 1. 83 ; § 153.

lār *f.* learning 1. 13, teaching 1. 11, study 1. 68.

lārēow *m.* teacher 1. 22, 4. 69.

lēad *n.* lead 2. 20.

lēaf *f.* leave, permission 4. 30.

lēan *sv.* 6 to blame § 186.

leax *m.* salmon 5. 61.

leccan *wv.* 1 to moisten § 195.

lecgan *wv.* 1 to lay 4. 74 ; §§ 81, 193, 197.

Ledengereord *n.* the Latin language 5. 16.

lēfan *see* lȳfan.

leng *see* lange.

lengest *see* lang, lange.

lengra *see* lang.

lēode *m. pl.* people § 110.

lēof *adj.* dear, beloved 4. 5, welcome 5. 8, (as title of address) Sir 5. 36 ; §§ 118, 124.

lēogan *sv.* 2 ; 3 *sing. pres.* līehþ to tell lies § 90.

lēoht *adj.* light, bright 2. 29.

lēon *sv.* 1 to lend § 166.

leornian, liornian *wv.* 2 to learn 1. 45, 4. 44 ; §§ 12, 32, 196.

leornung, liornung *f.* learning 5. 7; study 1. 64.

lesan *sv.* 5 to gather § 182.

lētanīa *m.* litany 5. 69.

libban, lybban *wv.* 3 to live 3. 10 ; §§ 45, 197.

liogan *sv.* 5 ; 3 *sing. pres.* ligeþ, līþ ; *pret. pl.* lāgon to lie, lie down 2. 29 ; §§ 28, 29, 64, 83, 89, 184.

līcian *wv.* 2 *impers.* to please 4. 61.

līcuma *m.* body § 94.

ligeþ *see* licgan.

liornian, liornung *see* leornian, leornung.

lītle *see* lȳtle.

līþan *sv.* 1 to go §§ 77, 165.

loc *n.* lock, bar 2. 26.

lofsang *m.* hymn of praise 5. 68.

lond, longe *see* land, lange.

lopystre *f.* lobster 5. 63.

lufian *wv.* 2 to love 1. 27 ; §§ 55 196.

lufigend *m.* lover 4. 81.

luflīce *adv.* lovingly 1. 2 ; § 147.

lufu *f.* love 4. 64.

lūs *f.* louse § 113.

lūtian *wv.* 2 to lurk, lie hidden 5. 25.

lybban *see* libban.

lȳfan, lēfan *wv.* 1 to allow 1. 28, 4. 66.

lȳt *adv. ;* *comp.* lǣs ; *superl.* lǣst little § 153.

lȳtel *adj. ;* *comp.* lǣssa ; *superl.* lǣst little 1. 34, 2. 27 ; §§ 65, 90, 125.

lȳtle, lītle *adv.* a little 4. 66.

mā *see* micle.

mǣd *f.* meadow § 109.

mǣden *n.* maiden 4. 12, 19.

mǣg *v. ;* *pl.* magon ; *pret.* meahte I can, am able 1. 20, 78, I may 4. 84 ; §§ 210, 211.

mǣg *m. ;* *pl.* māgas kinsman § 28.

mǣg(e)þ *f.* maiden § 114.

mǣgþ *f.* tribe, nation 2. 5.

mǣsse *f.* mass 5. 70.

mǣsseprīost *m.* mass-priest 1. 76.

mǣst *see* micel, micle.

magon *see* mǣg.

magu *m.* son § 111.

man, mon *indef. pron.* one 1. 13, 39 ; §§ 145, 233.

man *v.* I think §§ 199, 207.

mān *adj.* evil § 8.

mancus *m.* a coin worth thirty silver pence 1. 81 n.

manig, monig *adj. pron.* many 1. 18, 70, 5. 65 ; §§ 71, 119, 123, 227.

manigfeald *adj.* various, manifold 1. 71.

man(n), mon(n) *m. ;* *dat. sing. and nom. pl.* men(n) man 1. 63, 82, 3. 13 ; §§ 8, 24, 40, 102, 113.

māra *see* micel.

maþelian *wv.* 2 to speak § 14.

māþ(þ)um *m. ;* *gen. pl.* māþma treasure 1. 32.

māwan *sv.* 7 to mow § 190.

max *m.* net 5. 43.

mē *see* ic.

meahte *see* mæg.

meduma, medema *adv.* midway § 127.

meltan *sv.* 3 to melt § 173.

menigeo, menigu *f.* multitude 1. 33; § 109.

men(n) *see* man(n).

me(o)du *m.* mead § 111.

meol(u)c *f.* milk § 113.

meowle *f.* maiden § 56.

meregrota *m.* pearl 2. 14.

mereswȳn *n.* porpoise, dolphin 2. 12, 5. 61.

metan *sv.* 5 to measure § 180.

mētan *wv.* 1 ; *pp.* gemēt, gemēted to find 2. 21, 3. 46 ; § 66.

mete *m.* food 5. 48.

metod *m.* creator § 108.

micel, mycel *adj.* ; *dat. sing.* myccle great 1. 33, 2. 3, 3. 11 ; *comp.* māra 1. 50 ; *superl.* mǣst 2. 3 ; §§ 3, 104, 119, 125.

micle, mycele *adv.* greatly, by far 2. 32 ; *comp. w. gen.* mā more 1. 50 ; *superl.* mǣst most §§ 3, 149, 153.

mid *prep. w. dat.* with 1. 42, by 2. 24, in 1. 10.

mid(d) *adj.* ; *superl.* mid(e)mest middle ; **on middre nihte** in the middle of the night 2. 29 ; §§ 120, 127.

middæg *m.* midday, sext 5. 71.

middangeard *m.* earth 2. 28, 33.

mid-þȳ-þe, mid-þī-þe *cj. w. ind.* when 4. 1, 22.

mil *f.* mile 2. 4.

mildheortnes(s) *f.* mercy, compassion 3. 23.

mīn(e) *see* ic.

mislic *adj.* various 1. 71.

mis(s)enlic *adj.* various, different 2. 7, 12.

mōd *n.* heart, mind 1. 42, 4. 64.

mōdor *f.* mother § 115.

mon *see* man(n) *m.*, man *pron.*

mōnaþ *m.* month § 114.

monig *see* manig.

monn *see* man(n).

morgen *m.* morning 2. 31.

mōt *v.* ; *pret.* mōste I may 4. 66 ; § 209.

moþþe *f.* moth § 13.

munuc *m.* monk 5. 13 ; § 11.

murcnung *f.* sorrow 4. 30.

murnan *sv.* 3 to mourn § 176.

mūs *f.* mouse § 113.

mus(cu)le *f.* mussel 2. 13, 5. 62.

myccle, mycel(e) *see* micel, micle.

myltystre *f.* prostitute 3. 42.

myne *m.* minnow 5. 55.

mynster *n.* church 1. 83.

nā *adv.* not 4. 44, 5. 80.

nǣdl, nēþl *f.* needle § 107.

næfde = ne hæfde § 94.

nǣfre *adv.* never 3. 39, 40.

næfþ = ne hæfþ 4. 44.

nǣnig *pron.* no one § 145.

nǣnne *see* nān.

nǣre(n), nǣron, næs = ne wǣre(n), ne wǣron, ne wæs §§ 94, 213.

næs *adv.* by no means 5. 6.

nāht *see* nāwiht.

nāhwæþer *pron.* neither of two ; *cj.* neither ; nōhwæþer ne . . . ne neither . . . nor 1. 27 ; § 143.

nam *see* niman.

nama *m.* name, reputation 1. 28, 81.

nān *adj.* no ; *acc. sing. m.* nǣnne 1. 45, 65 ; *pron.* no one ; §§ 145, 222.

nānwuht *pron. w. gen.* nothing 1. 35.

nāst, nāt = ne wāst, ne wāt 4. 7, 45 ; §§ 94, 200.

nāwiht, nāht, nōht *pron.* nothing ; *adv.* not 1. 18 ; § 145.

ne *adv.* not 1. 20 ; nor 4. 10 ; ne . . . ne neither . . . nor 2. 16 ; §§ 213, 222.

nēah *adj.* (rare in positive) ; *comp.* nēarra ; *superl.* nīehst, nȳhst near §§ 32, 124.

nēah *adv.* ; *comp.* nēar ; *superl.* nīehst, nȳhst near 2. 28 ; § 151.

neaht *see* niht.

nēan *adv.* from near § 151.

nearu *adj.* narrow § 121.

nēat *n.* ox, cow 2. 8.

neddre *f.* adder 2. 22.

nefa *m.* nephew § 112.

nellan = ne willan 5. 9 ; § 216.

nemnan *wv.* 1 ; *pp.* **genemned** to name, call 3. 20, 26.

nēod *f.* zeal, pleasure 4. 17.

neom = ne eom 5. 36.

nerian *wv.* 1 to save §§ 72, 81, 193.

nīedbeþearf *adj.* necessary 1. 59.

nigon *num.* nine § 128.

nigontēoþa *num.* nineteenth § 128.

nigontīene *num.* nineteen § 128.

nigoþa *num.* ninth § 128.

niht, neaht *f.* night 2. 29, 30 ; **nihtes** by night ; §§ 113, 225.

niht-sangc *m.* compline 5. 74.

niman *sv.* 4 ; *pret. sing.* **nam, nōm** ; *pret. pl.* **nōmon** ; *pp.* **(ge)numen** to take 4. 50, to catch, gather 2. 12 ; §§ 23, 25, 26, 179.

nis = ne is § 213.

niþan, nioþan *adv.* below §§ 127, 151.

niþer *adv.* down § 151.

niþerra *adj. comp.* lower ; *superl.* **niþemest** lowest § 127.

nōht *see* **nāwiht.**

nōhwæþer *see* **nāhwæþer.**

nolde, noldon = ne wolde, ne woldon 1. 41, 3. 37 ; §§ 94, 216.

nōm(on) *see* **niman.**

nōn *n.* nones 5. 72.

norþ *adv.* northwards 2. 4 ; § 127.

norþdǣl *m.* northern part, north 2. 2, 28.

norþerra, nyrþra *adj. comp.* more northern ; *superl.* **norþmest** § 127.

nosu *f.* nose §§ 84, 111.

notu *f.* employment 1. 65.

nū *adv.* now 1. 14, 21.

numen *see* **niman.**

nȳhst *see* **nēah.**

nyl(l)e, nyllan = ne wil(l)e, ne willan §§ 58, 216, 222.

nys = ne is 5. 24.

nyste = ne wiste § 58.

of *prep. w. dat.* from 1. 17, 2. 15, by 5. 40, with 3. 15.

ofdūne *adv.* down § 150.

ofslēan *sv.* 6 ; *pret. sing.* **ofslōh ofslōg ;** *pp.* **ofslægen** to kill 3. 29, 36 ; § 119.

oft *adv.* ; *superl.* **oftost** often 1. 3, 24 ; § 152.

on *prep. w. acc. or dat.* in 1. 6, 13, into 1. 3, 18, on 3. 2, at 5. 23, during 5. 32, against 3. 19, because of 3. 18, 4. 32, of the value of 1. 81 ; **on dæg** daily 5. 81.

onbelǣdan *wv.* 1 to inflict upon 5.10.

oncnāwan *sv.* 7 to admit 4. 46.

ond *see* **and.**

ondrǣdan *sv.* 7 to fear §§ 188, 189.

onfēng *see* **onfōn.**

onfindan *sv.* 3 to discover § 84.

onfōn *sv.* 7 ; *pret.* **onfēng** to receive 3. 36.

ongēan *adv.* opposite 2. 5, again 4. 4.

ongegen *prep. w. dat.* opposite 2. 4.

ongemang *prep. w. dat.* among 1. 70.

ongietan, ongiotan *sv.* 5 to understand, perceive 1. 35 ; §§ 14, 181.

onginnan *sv.* 3 ; *pret. sing.* **ongan ;** *pret. pl.* **ongunnon** to begin 4. 37, 38.

ongiotan *see* **ongietan.**

onlūtan *sv.* 2 to incline 1. 42.

onman *v.* I esteem § 207.

onsacan *sv.* 6 to strive against § 14.

onsendan *wv.* 1 to send 1. 80.

onstāl *m.* supply 1. 22.

onw(e)ald *m.* power, authority 1. 6, 8.

onweg *adv.* away 2. 23 ; §§ 14, 150.

ōra *m.* ore 2. 20.

ostre *f.* oyster 5. 61.

oþ *prep. w. acc.* until 1. 65.

ōþer *adj.* other 1. 27, 54 ; *num.* second ; *pron.* another 1. 87 ; §§ 122, 128, 134, 227.

oþfæstan *wv.* 1 to set (to a task) 1. 64.

oþfeallan *sv.* 7 to decline 1. 15, 49.

oþþe *cj.* or 1. 17, 86.

oxa *m.* ; *pl.* **oxan, oexen, oxon** ox 5. 24, 26 ; §§ 11, 112.

oxanhyrde *m.* ox-herd 5. 18.

pæþ *m.* ; *pl.* **paþas** path §§ 16, 29.

peni(n)g *m.* penny § 100.

plega *m.* play, game 4. 9.

plegian *wv.* 2 to act 4. 59.

plēon *sv.* 5 to risk § 183.
plōg *m.* a measure of land § 13.
prīm *n.* prime 5. 68.
pund *n.* pound 4. 70.
pyffan *wv.* 1 to puff § 13.

rǣcan *wv.* 1 to reach § 195.
rǣdan, rēdan *sv.* 7 to advise §§ 188, 189.
rǣding *f.* reading 5. 14.
raþe *adv.* quickly 3. 27.
rēaf *n.* treasure 4. 72.
rēcan *wv.* 1 to care 5. 5.
reccan *wv.* 1 to narrate § 195.
reccelēas *adj.* careless 1. 48.
regen *m.* rain 2. 16.
rēwyt *n.* rowing 5. 58.
rīce *n.* sovereignty 1. 21, kingdom, country 1. 80.
rīdan *sv.* 1 to ride §§ 11, 13.
riht *adj.* correct 5. 5.
rihte *adv.* correctly 5. 2.
rōwan *sv.* 7 to row § 190.

sǣ *mf.* sea 4. 18, 5. 57 ; § 62.
sǣcocc *m.* cockle 5. 62.
sǣd *n.* seed § 28.
sǣgest *see* **secgan.**
sǣwiht *fn.* creature living in the sea 2. 10.
same *adv.* similarly ; **swǣ same** similarly 1. 55.
sang *m.* singing, song 4. 37.
sang *see* **singan.**
sār *n.* wound, grief 4. 26.
sārlic *adj.* sad 4. 6.
sārness *f.* grief 4. 35.
sāwan *sv.* 7 to sow § 190.
sāwol *f.* soul §§ 69, 109.
sāwon *see* **sēon** *sv.* 5.
sc(e)acan *sv.* 6 to shake §§ 9, 185.
sc(e)ādan *sv.* 7 to divide § 189.
sceadu *f.* shadow § 93.
sc(e)afan *sv.* 6 to shave § 185.
sceal *v.* ; *pret. pl.* **sc(e)oldon** I must 1. 14, 5. 38 ; §§ 13, 38, 206, 237.
scē(a)p *n.* sheep 2. 8 ; § 53.
scear *mn.* ploughshare 5. 27.
scearn *n.* dung 5. 34.
scencan *wv.* 1 to pour out § 194.

sceoldon *see* **sceal.**
sceort *adj.* ; *comp.* **scyrtra ;** *superl.* **scyrtest** short §§ 38, 124.
scēota *m.* trout 5. 55.
scēotan *sv.* 2 to shoot § 167.
scēowyrhta *m.* shoemaker 5. 20.
scēp *see* **scē(a)p.**
scēphyrde *m.* shepherd 5. 18.
sceþþan *sv.* 6 to injure § 187.
scieppan *sv.* 6. to create § 187.
scieran *sv.* 4 to cut §§ 36, 178.
scip, scyp *n.* ship 5. 43 ; §§ 46, 108.
scōh *m.* shoe § 13.
scrīdan *see* **scrȳdan.**
scrīþan *sv.* 1 to go § 165.
scrūd *n.* garment, clothing 5. 41 ; § 113.
scrȳdan, scrīdan *wv.* 1 to dress, clothe 3. 28, 4. 49.
scūfan *sv.* 2 to push § 170.
scū(w)a *m.* shadow § 63.
scyp *see* **scip.**
sē *pron. art.* ; *instr.* **þȳ, þon** that, the 1. 85, *rel.* who, which 1. 81, he, it § 230 ; **on þon** so 2. 31 ; **þȳ . . . þȳ** the . . . the 1. 50 ; § 138.
sealde(st) *see* **sellan.**
sealtere *m.* salt-worker 5. 20.
sealtsēaþ *m.* salt spring 2. 18.
sēc(e)an *wv.* 1 ; *pret.* **sōhte** to seek 1. 13, 4. 84 ; §§ 40, 195.
secgan *wv.* 3 ; *2 sing. pres.* **sǣgest** ; *imper. sing.* **sege** to say 5. 22, to tell 4. 15 ; §§ 13, 64, 83, 99, 197.
sēfte *adj.* soft § 146
seglan, siglan *wv.* 1 to sail § 194.
sel(d)lic *adj.* strange § 97.
seldon *adv.* seldom 5. 58.
sēlest *adj. superl.* best 3. 27 ; § 125.
self, sylf, silf *adj.* himself 4. 56, same 2. 28 ; (*strengthening pron.*) 1. 27 ; §§ 140, 230.
sellan, syllan, sillan *wv.* 1 ; *imper. sing.* **syle** ; *pret.* **sealde** to give 1. 25, 3. 3, 16, 4. 45 ; §§ 32, 195.
sēlra *adj. comp.* better § 125.
sendan *wv.* 1 to send 3. 13 ; § 101.
sēo *see* **sē.**

sē(o)c *adj.* sick § 54.
seofon *num.* seven 5. 14, 69 ;
§ 128.
seofontēoþa *num.* seventeenth
§ 128.
seofontīene *num.* seventeen § 128.
seofoþa *num.* seventh § 128.
seolfor, siolfor *n.* silver 2. 21, 4. 71 ;
§ 45.
seolh *m.* seal 2. 11 ; § 108.
seolm, sealm *m.* psalm 5. 69.
sēon *sv.* 1 to sift § 166.
sēon *sv.* 5 ; *pret. pl.* sāwon to see
§§ 13, 28, 63, 98, 183.
sēoþan *sv.* 2 to boil § 168.
seoþþan *see* siþþan.
setl *n.* seat 4. 6.
settan *wv.* 1 to put, place 4. 49,
5. 88 ; §§ 11, 40, 81, 90, 193.
sī *see* bēon.
sibb *f.* peace 1. 8.
sīe(n), siendon *see* bēon.
si(e)x, syx *num.* six §§ 50, 128.
si(e)xta, syxta *num.* sixth § 128.
si(e)xtēoþa *num.* sixteenth § 128.
si(e)xtīene *num.* sixteen § 128.
si(e)xtig *num.* sixty § 128.
si(e)xtigoþa *num.* sixtieth § 128.
sigor *m.* victory § 117.
silf, sillan *see* self, sellan.
sīn *pron., reflex,* his, its § 137.
sindon *see* bēon.
singan, sincgan, syngan *sv.* 3 ;
pret. sing. sang ; *pret. pl.*
sungon to sing 5. 13, 67, 74 ;
§ 13.
sint, sīo *see* bēon, sē.
si(o)du *m.* custom, morality 1. 8 ;
§ 111.
siolfor *see* seolfor.
sittan *sv.* 5 to sit 4. 6 ; §§ 11, 29,
90, 159, 160, 162, 184.
sīþ *adv.* late § 127.
sīþemest *adj. superl.* latest § 127.
sīþþan, seoþþan, syþþan *adv.*
afterwards 1. 66 ; *cj.* when 1. 55;
§§ 45, 65, 67.
slǣpan *sv.* 7 ; *pret. pl.* slēpon,
slǣpton to sleep 5. 71 ; § 189.
slāw *adj.* slow § 121.
slēan *sv.* 6 to strike §§ 15, 34, 64, 77,
98, 156, 162, 186.
slēpon *see* slǣpan.

smēþe *adj.* smooth § 146.
smōþ *adj.* smooth § 146.
smōþe *adv.* smoothly § 146.
snā(w) *m.* snow § 87.
snīþan *sv.* 1 to cut § 165.
sōft *adj.* soft § 146.
sōfte *adv.* ; *comp.* sēft softly §§ 22,
146, 153.
sōhte *see* sēc(e)an.
sōna *adv.* at once, immediately
1. 46 ; sōna swā as soon as
4. 36 ; § 148.
sōþlīce *adv.* indeed 3. 5, 6, truth-
fully 4. 21.
spanan *sv.* 6 to entice § 185.
spannan *sv.* 7 to fasten, clasp §§ 185,
190.
spēd *f.* wealth, riches 1. 63, 3. 42.
speld *n.* splinter § 117.
spēow *see* spōwan.
spere *n.* spear § 110.
spitu *m.* spit § 111.
spor *n.* track, footprint 1. 42.
spōwan *sv.* 7 ; *pret.* spēow *impers.*
to succeed 1. 9 ; §§ 57, 190.
sprǣc *f.* speech 4. 13, 21.
sprecan *sv.* 5 ; 2 *sing. pres.*
sprycst, spricst to speak, say
5. 2, 11 ; § 13.
sprot(t) *m.* sprat, small fish 5. 56.
sprycst *see* sprecan.
spurnan *sv.* 3 to spurn § 176.
spyri(ge)an *wv.* 1 to go, follow
1. 40 ; § 193.
spyrte *f.* wicker pot 5. 44.
stæfn, stefn *f.* voice 4. 57.
stān *m.* stone, precious stone 2. 21 ;
§ 108.
standan *sv.* 6 ; *pret. pl.* stōdon to
stand 1. 32 ; § 13, 185.
stearc *adj.* severe 5. 25.
stede *m.* place § 110.
stelan *sv.* 4 to steal § 177.
stellan *wv.* 1 to place § 195.
steorfan *sv.* 3 to die § 175.
steppan *sv.* 6 to step § 187.
stille *adj.* still, quiet 4. 13.
stilnes(s) *f.* peace, quiet 1. 62, 4. 53.
stiria *m.* sturgeon 5. 61.
stōdon *see* standan.
stōw *f.* place 1. 37, 2. 8.
strang *adj.* ; *comp.* strengra;
superl. strengest strong § 124.

streccan *wv.* 1 to stretch § 195.
stregdan *sv.* 3 to strew § 171.
strengþu, *f.* strength § 109.
strīenan *wv.* 1 to acquire § 40.
studu *f.* pillar § 113.
styccemǣlum *adv.* here and there § 149.
styric *n.* calf 3. 29.
sulh *f.* ; *dat. sing.* **syl** plough 5. 24, 27 ; § 113.
sum *adj.* ; *sing.* a certain, a 1. 57, 3. 6 ; *pl.* some 1. 59, 2. 8 ; *pron.* someone §§ 145, 219.
sumor *m.* ; *dat. sing.* **sumera** summer 2. 29, 32.
sungon *see* **singan.**
sunne *f.* sun 2. 16.
sunu *m.* son 3. 6, 9 ; §§ 69, 105, 111.
sūþ *adv.* southwards § 127.
sūþan *adv.* from the south ; **be sūþan** south of 1. 20.
sūþdǣl *m.* southern part, south 2. 5, 33.
swā, swǣ *adv. cj.* so, such 4. 6, as 1. 23, in such a way 4. 50, to such an extent 1. 48 ; **swā swā** as 3. 2 ; **swā . . . swā** as . . . as 5. 52, as . . . so 2. 17 ; **swā þæt** so that 2. 29.
swæþ *n.* track, footprint 1. 39.
swā-hwæt-swā *pron.* whatever 4. 26, 66.
swāpan *sv.* 7 to sweep § 190.
swā-wylce-swā *adj. pl.* whatever 5. 56.
swēg *m.* noise, sound 3. 33, music 4. 38.
swēgcræft *m.* musical performance 4. 38, 43.
swelc, swilc, swylc *pron. adj* such 5. 63 ; § 145.
swelce, swilce, swylce *cj. w. subj.* as if 1. 36; **ēac swilce, swylce ēac** likewise 2. 9, 4. 79.
swelgan *sv.* 3 to swallow § 173.
swellan *sv.* 3 to swell § 173.
sweltan *sv.* 3 to die § 173.
sweord, swurd *n.* sword § 59.
sweostor, swostor, swustor *f.* sister §§ 48, 59, 115.
sweotol, swutol *adj.* clear, evident 2. 31 ; §§ 48, 146.
sweotole *adv.* clearly § 146.

swerian *sv.* 6 to swear § 187.
swēte *adj.* sweet § 146.
swice *adj.* deceitful § 120.
swīgende (*pres. part. of rare v.* **swīgan**) remaining silent 4. 41.
swīge *f.* silence 4. 53.
swīgian *wv.* 2 to be silent 4. 39.
swilc, swilce *see* **swelc, swelce.**
swingell *f.* ; *acc. pl.* **swincgla** blow, chastisement 5. 10.
swīþe, swȳþe *adv.* very 1. 2, 61, 2. 14 ; **swīþe swīþe** very much indeed 1. 43.
swōgan *sv.* 7 to sound § 190.
swōt *adj.* sweet § 146.
swōte *adv.* sweetly § 146.
swustor, swutol *see* **sweostor, sweotol.**
swylc, swylce *see* **swelc, swelce.**
swymman, swimman *sv.* 3 to swim 5. 56.
swȳn, swīn *n.* swine, pig 3. 14, 15.
swȳþe, sȳ *see* **swīþe, bēon.**
syl *see* **sulh.**
syle, syllan ; **sylf** *see* **sellan** ; self.
symle *adv.* always 3. 43.
synd(on), syngan *see* **bēon, singan.**
syngian *wv.* 2 to sin, offend 3. 19, 25.
synt *see* **bēon.**
sȳþerra, sūþerra *adj. comp.* more southern ; *superl.* **sūþmest** § 127.
syþþan *see* **siþþan.**

tǣcan *wv.* 1 to teach 5. 2 ; § 195.
tǣlan *wv.* 1 to blame 4. 41.
tælhg, telg *m.* dye 2. 16.
tēah *see* **tēon** *sv.* 2.
tēar, tæhher *m.* tear 4. 22 ; § 82.
tela *adv.* well § 148.
tellan *wv.* 1 to count § 195.
temian *wv.* 1 to tame § 193.
teohhian, tiohhian *wv.* 2 to think § 32.
tēon *sv.* 1 to accuse §§ 32, 166.
tēon *sv.* 2 ; *pret. sing.* **tēah** ; *pp.* **getogen** to draw ; to instruct 4. 63 ; **forþ tēah** had recourse to 4. 59 ; § 169.
tēond *m.* accuser § 116.
tēoþa *num.* tenth § 128.
ticcen *n.* kid 3. 40.

tīd *f.* time 1. 5, hour 5. 14.

tīen *num.* ten § 128.

tīma *m.* appropriate time 5. 75.

timbran *wv.* 1 to build § 194.

timbrian *wv.* 2 to build 2. 26.

tō *prep. w. dat.* to 1. 21, 3. 7, towards 4. 23, as 5. 48 ; (*w. gerund to express purpose etc.*) 1. 60 ; **tō lǣne** on loan 1. 86 ; **tō þǣm** . . . **þæt** in order that 1. 24 ; *adv.* too 4. 15.

tōbecuman *sv.* 4 to come about 3. 2.

tō-dæg *adv.* today 3. 3, 5. 64 ; § 150.

tōdǣlan *wv.* 1 to separate, divide 2. 19.

tōforan *prep. w. dat.* before, in front of 5. 88.

tōgenȳdan *wv.* 1 to compel 5. 10.

torr *m.* tower 2. 26.

tōþ *m.* tooth §§ 22, 96, 113.

trēo(w) *n.* tree 2. 7 ; §§ 56, 62, 87, 108.

trum *adj.* strong 2. 26.

trymian *wv.* 1 to strengthen § 193.

tū *see* **twēgen**.

tūn *m* .estate, farm 3. 14.

tunge *f.* tongue § 112.

turf *f.* turf § 113.

twā *see* **twēgen**.

twēgen, tū, twā *num.* two 2. 4, 3. 6, 4. 70 ; §§ 128, 130.

twelf *num.* twelve § 128.

twelfta *num.* twelfth § 128.

twentig *num.* twenty 4. 72 ; § 128.

twentigoþa *num.* twentieth § 128.

twifeald *adj.* twofold § 135.

twiwa *adv.* twice § 148.

þā *adj. pron. pl.* these, those 1. 67, these things 5. 67 ; **þā þe** who, which 1. 37, 59 ; § 138.

þā *adv.* then 1. 5, 9, 3. 6 ; **þā þā** when 1. 20 ; **þā** . . . **þā** when . . . then 1. 30 ; § 220.

þǣm, þǣne *see* **sē**.

þænne *see* **þonne**.

þǣr, þār *adv.* there 2. 22, 3. 10 ; **þǣr þǣr** where 1. 25 ; §§ 11, 151, 220.

þǣra *see* **þā** *pron.*

þǣre, þǣs *see* **sē**.

þæt *cj.* that 1. 2, in order that 4. 20.

þæt *pron. art.* it 2. 4, the § 138.

þām *see* **sē, þā** *pron.*

þancian *wv.* 2 *w. dat. gen.* to thank 4. 32 ; § 13.

þancung *f.* thankfulness 5. 86.

þār *see* **þǣr**.

þāra, þāre *see* **þā** *pron.*, **sē**.

þās *see* **þes**.

þe *rel. pron. indecl.* who 1. 6, which 1. 59 ; *cj.* when 1. 66 ; **þe** . . . **þe** (whether) . . . or 2. 30.

þē *see* **þū**.

þēah *adv.* nevertheless 4. 14 ; *cj. w. subj.* although 4. 13.

þēahhwæþere *adv.* nevertheless 5. 15.

þearf *v.* I need §§ 199, 204.

þearle *adv.* hard, severely 5. 23, very much 4. 61.

þēaw *m.* custom, habit ; *pl.* virtues, morality 1. 29.

þeccan *wv.* 1 to cover § 195.

þegnian *wv.* 2 to serve § 99.

þenc(e)an *wv.* 1 ; *pret.* **þōhte** to think §§ 9, 13, 21, 195.

þēning *f.* mass-book 1. 16.

þēon *sv.* 1 to prosper § 166.

þēos *see* **þes**.

þēo(w), þīo(w) *m.* servant 1. 33, 3. 34 ; **þēow mann** servant 4. 73 ; § 108.

þēowian *wv.* 2 to serve, work for 3. 39.

þerscan *sv.* 3 to thresh § 171.

þes *adj. and pron.* this 3. 30, 4. 8 ; §§ 139, 227.

þicgan *sv.* 5 to receive § 184.

þider *adv.* thither § 151.

þīn *see* **þū**.

þincan *see* **þyncan**.

þing(c) *n.* thing 4. 47, 73 ; *pl.* possessions 3. 9 ; § 13.

þīod, þēod *f.* people, nation 1. 57.

þīos *see* **þes**.

þīo(w) *see* **þēo(w)**.

þīowotdōm *m.* service 1. 12.

þis, þisne, þissa, þisse, þis(s)es, þis(s)um *see* **þes**.

þon *see* **sē**.

þonan *adv.* thence § 151.

þonc *m.* thanks 1. 21, 84.
þone *see* sē.
þonne, þænne *adv. cj.* then 2. 22, when 5. 75, than 2. 33, 5. 8.
þrēotēoþa *num.* thirteenth § 128.
þrēotīene *num.* thirteen § 128.
þridda *num.* third § 128.
þrī(e), þrīo, þrēo *num.* three §§ 128, 131.
þrifeald *adj.* threefold § 135.
þrītig, þrittig *num.* thirty 2. 25 ; § 128.
þrītigoþa *num.* thirtieth § 128.
þrittig *see* þrītig.
þrūh *f.* trough § 113.
þū *pron.* thou 1. 23 ; §§ 136, 137.
þūhte *see* þyncan.
þurh *prep. w. acc.* by means of, with the help of 1. 56, through-out 2. 19.
þus *adv.* thus 4. 73, 75.
þūsend *n.* thousand §§ 128, 133.
þwēan *sv.* 6 to wash § 186.
þweorh *adj.* perverse § 118.
þȳ *see* sē.
þȳn *wv.* 1 to press § 194.
þyncan, þincan *wv.* 1 ; *pret.* þūhte *impers.* to seem 1. 58, 4. 15 ; §§ 21, 40, 78, 195.
þyslic *pron.* such § 145.
þysum *see* þes.
þȳwan *wv.* 1 to drive 5. 24, 30.

ufan *adv.* above § 127.
uferra *adj. comp.* higher ; *superl.* ufemest § 127.
ūhtsang *m.* matins 5. 67.
unclǣne *adj.* unclean 5. 46, 47.
uncūþ *adj.* unknown 1. 83.
under *prep. w. dat.* under, in 2. 28, 5. 82 ; § 64.
understandan, understondan *sv.* 6 to understand 1. 17, 4. 20.
undertīd *f.* tierce 5. 70.
ungeāra *adv.* recently § 149.
ungecnāwen *ppl. adj.* unknown 4. 60.
ungelǣred *adj.* ignorant 5. 2.
ungewunelic *adj.* unwonted, un-usual 4. 60.
unrīm *n.* countless number 2. 27.

unrōt *adj.* sad 4. 14.
ūp(p) *adv.* above, up § 151.
uppan, uppon *prep. w. acc.* upon 4. 49 ; *adv.* above § 151.
uppe *adv.* on high, up § 151.
uppon *see* uppan.
ūre, ūs(er) *see* wē.
ūt *adv.* out 4. 69, abroad 1. 9 ; §§ 127, 151.
ūtan *adv.* from outside § 151.
ūtanbordes *adv.* abroad 1. 13.
ūte *adv.* outside, abroad 1. 14 ; § 151.
ūterra *adj. comp.* outer ; *superl.* ūt(e)mest § 127.
utun *v.* let us 3. 29n.
ūtweorpan, ūtwyrpan *sv.* 3 to throw away 5. 47.

wadan *sv.* 6 to go § 185.
wǣdl, wēþl *f.* poverty § 107.
wǣdla *m.* pauper 3. 12.
wǣre(n) *see* wesan.
wǣrlīce *adv.* warily 5. 77.
wǣron, wæs *see* wesan.
wæsp, wæps *m.* wasp § 92.
wæstm *mn.* fruit 2. 7.
wæter *n.* water, expanse of water 2. 10, 18 ; § 108.
wæterian *wv.* 2 to provide water for 5. 34.
wamb *f.* stomach 3. 15.
wana *adj. indecl.* wanting, less 2. 25.
wange *n.* cheek § 112.
wāt *v.* ; 2 *sing. pres.* wāst ; *infin.* witan ; *pret. pl.* wiston I know 1. 34, 4. 45, 5. 80 ; to wiotonne to know 1. 60 ; §§ 198, 200.
wāwan *sv.* 7 to blow § 190.
waxgeorn *adj.* greedy 5. 87.
wē *pron.* ; *gen.* ūser, ūre ; *acc. dat.* ūs we 1. 21, 26, 42 ; §§ 96, 136, 137.
wealcan *sv.* 7 to roll § 190.
weald *m.* wood § 111.
wealdan *sv.* 7 to wield § 190.
wealdend *m.* ruler § 116.
wealhstod *m.* interpreter 1. 56.
weall *m.* wall 2. 25.
weallan *sv.* 7 to boil § 190.

wearþ *see* **weorþan.**

weaxan *sv.* 7 to grow § 44, 190.

weccan *wv.* 1 to awake § 195.

wecg *m.* (mass of) metal 2. 20.

weg *m.* way § 89.

wel *adv.* well 4. 44, with ease 1. 66 ; § 153.

wela *m.* wealth, riches 1. 38, 41.

welhwǣr *adv.* everywhere 1. 84.

welig *adj.* rich 2. 6, 4. 31.

welwillendness *f.* benevolence, good will 4. 33.

wēnan *wv.* 1 to think 1. 18, to expect 1. 47 ; § 194.

wendan *wv.* 1 to translate 1. 46, 53.

wēoh, wīh *m.* idol § 54.

weolcscyll *f.* whelk, shellfish 2. 13.

weoloc *m.* whelk 2. 15.

weoloc-rēad *adj.* scarlet, purple 2. 15.

we(o)rc, weork *n.* work, task 5. 12, 22 ; §§ 13, 54.

weorpan *sv.* 3 ; 1 *sing. pres.* **weorpe, wyrpe** to throw 5. 43, 44 ; §§ 12, 32, 175.

weorþan *sv.* 3 ; *pret.* **wearþ ;** *pp.* **geworden** to be, become 1. 48, to happen 4. 53 ; §§ 80, 155, 175, 233.

wēpan *sv.* 7 to weep §§ 160, 190.

wer *m.* man § 20.

werod, weryd *n.* crowd, multitude 3. 34, troop § 69.

wesan *v.* ; *pret. sing.* **wæs ;** *pl.* **wǣron** to be 1. 10, 69, 5. 9 ; §§ 29, 155, 182, 213, 233.

west *adv.* westwards § 127.

westdǣl *m.* western part, west 2. 2.

westerra *adj. comp.* more westerly ; *superl.* **westmest** § 127.

wīfmann, wimman *m.* woman §§ 65, 90, 113.

wīg *n.* war 1. 10 ; § 8.

wiga *m.* warrior § 8.

wīgend *m.* warrior § 116.

wiht, wuht *fm.* thing § 59.

wilde *adj.* wild §§ 106, 120, 122, 123, 137.

willa *m.* will, pleasure 3. 2.

willan, wyllan *v.* ; *pret.* **wolde** to wish 1. 67, 4. 28, to intend 1. 23 : §§ 9, 58, 64, 212, 216, 237.

wilnung *f.* desire 1. 49 ; § 109.

wīn *n.* wine § 8.

wind *m.* wind § 18.

windan *sv.* 3 ; *pp.* **wunden** to twist § 119.

wine *m.* friend §§ 8, 68, 110.

winewincle *f.* winkle, shellfish 5. 62.

wīngeard *m.* vineyard 2. 9.

winsum *adj.* pleasant 4. 37, 56.

winter *m.* winter 2. 33, 5. 25.

wiota, wiotonne *see* **wita, wāt.**

wīs *adj.* wise, learned 1. 56.

wīsdōm *m.* wisdom, learning 1. 10, 13.

wiste, wiston *see* **wāt.**

wit *pron.* we two §§ 136, 137.

wita, wiota, wuta *m.* scholar 1. 3, 44 ; § 48.

witan *see* **wāt.**

wīte *n.* punishment, torment 1. 26 ; § 108.

wlæc *adj.* tepid § 118.

wlōh *f.* fringe § 113.

wolde, woldon *see* **willan.**

word *n.* word 1. 1, 73 ; §§ 13, 108.

woruld *f.* world 1. 26 ; § 48.

woruldcund *adj.* secular 1. 4.

woruldþing *n.* worldly affair 1. 23.

wrǣclice *adv.* in exile 3. 10.

wrǣstlian *wv.* 2 to wrestle § 65.

wrecan *sv.* 5 to avenge § 180.

wrēon *sv.* 1 to cover § 166.

wrītan *sv.* 1 to write, copy 1. 87 ; § 164.

wrīþan *sv.* 1 to twist § 165.

wudu *m.* wood §§ 48, 111.

wulf *m.* wolf §§ 13, 55, 84.

wunden *see* **windan.**

wundrian *wv.* 2 to wonder 1. 43.

wundrum *adv.* wonderfully § 149.

wurþian *wv.* 2 to honour 2. 24.

wurþlic *adj.* honoured 4. 6.

wyllan *see* **willan.**

wyllgespryng *n.* spring 2. 10.

wyrcan *wv.* 1 ; *pret.* **worhte ;** *pp.* **geworht** to make 2. 15 ; §§ 75, 195

wyrdan *wv.* 1 to injure, damage 2. 16.

wyrm, wurm *m.* serpent § 60.

wyrpe *see* **weorpan.**

wyrt *f.* vegetable 5. 85.

wyrþe *adj.* worthy 3. 20, 26.

yfel *adj.* ; *comp.* **wiersa, wyrsa, wursa** ; *superl.* **wier(re)st** evil ; *n.* evil 3. 5 ; §§ 60, 125.

yfele *adv.* badly, ill 4. 40 ; § 153.

yferra *adj. comp.* higher ; *superl.* **yfemest** § 127.

yldo *f.* age 2. 19.

yldra *see* eald.

ymb *prep. w. acc.* in, concerning 1. 11, 12.

ymbsittende *adj.* sitting near 4. 3, 51.

yppan *wv.* 1 to reveal, betray 5. 79.

yrþlin(c)g *m.* farm labourer 3. 17, 5. 22.

ys *see* bēon.

ȳterra *adj. comp.* outer ; *superl.* **ȳt(e)mest** § 127.

ytst *see* etan.